Gerry Adams –
A Biography

COLM KEENA

THE MERCIER PRESS

The Mercier Press Limited
4 Bridge Street, Cork
24 Lower Abbey Street, Dublin 1

© Colm Keena, 1990

British Library Cataloguing in Publication Data
Keena, Colm *1960–*
    Gerry Adams – a biography
    1. (Republic) Ireland. Politics. Adams, Gerry
    I. Title
    941.70824092

    ISBN 0 85342 906 5

To Pat and Delia

Thanks to John

The author and publisher would like to thank Grafton Books for
permission to quote from **Ten Men Dead** by David Beresford.

Printed in the Republic of Ireland

Contents

CONTENTS

Foreword

On 6 October 1988 Gerry Adams MP celebrated his 40th birthday. A large crowd of republicans gathered in a leisure centre in West Belfast to mark the occasion, men and women involved either in violence or political activity, or both, in their efforts to drive the British from Northern Ireland. A light-hearted 'This Is Your Life' show was performed for Adams, riddled with good-natured 'slagging'. Many of the people whom Adams would have liked to have had at that birthday celebration could not attend – either because they were in prison or because they were dead.

A real 'This Is Your Life' for Gerry Adams would have to be either a lengthy or a viciously-edited affair. A working-class Catholic from Belfast who left school early and now argues politics and theology with the political and religious leaders of Ireland. The alleged 'chief tactician' and for many the hated public face of an organisation responsible for so many deaths, but yet a committed Mass-going Catholic. A tall, bearded, pipe-smoking, reasonable debater and sensitive writer who has spent all his adult life considering the effects of a campaign of political violence and death. A popular local hero, local historian, local political representative who finds it so hurtful to be a figure of hate. A devoted family man. A man who has been imprisoned, beaten and tortured. A man who has lived his adult life surrounded by violent death.

Gerry Adams, according to the security forces, joined the IRA in the mid-sixties. In the early seventies he was Officer Commanding the 2nd (Ballymurphy) Battalion of the Belfast Brigade and later Officer Commanding of the Brigade, they say. At one period he and two other men are said to have been running the IRA, with Adams in charge of the campaign in Northern Ireland; and in the late seventies he is said to have spent a brief period as Chief of Staff. The British authorities however, although they would dearly like to, have never been able to provide evidence of Adams ever having been a member of this illegal organisation, or ever having been directly involved in any way in the campaign of violence conducted by that organisation. He himself denies that he is or ever was a member of the IRA.

He says he wishes he did not have to live through a period in Irish history that necessitated the use of violence, but that the continued British presence in Northern Ireland makes violence necessary and gives a mandate to the IRA for its actions. Republican violence is 'justifiable and morally correct', he says. The ending of the British presence in Ireland is a prerequisite for the ending of the armed conflict.

This book is an attempt to tell the story of Gerry Adams and try to understand why a former apprentice barman from a European member-state country in the closing decade of the 20th century, comes to be speaking such words.

1: Truce Maker

It was just under eight months after the introduction of internment that they finally caught up with him, one of the most wanted men in Belfast. The British army raided the house he had been using as a safe house, or billet as the republicans call them, on Harrowgate Street in the Beechmount area of West Belfast, on the night of Monday, 14 March 1972. He gave them a false name, Joseph McGuigan, but the soldiers were suspicious and they brought him to Springfield Road Barracks, then the main barracks in West Belfast. The prisoner almost had the army interrogators convinced he was who he said he was, but then they brought in an officer from the Royal Ulster Constabulary's Special Branch who knew him and identified him as Gerry Adams, well-known Belfast republican activist, prominent in the Ballymurphy area, suspected member of the Provisional IRA [PIRA] and Officer Commanding the 2nd (Ballymurphy) Battalion of that organisation's Belfast Brigade. He was to be taken to the notorious Palace Barracks, in the Hollywood suburb of Belfast. They put him into the back of an army personnel carrier and drove him through the city under heavy guard. The soldiers were excited – two other leading republicans had been caught that night, Brendan McNamee, said to be the commanding officer of A Company of the IRA's 2nd Battalion, and another man, said to be explosives officer with the Ardoyne Company of the 3rd Battalion.[1] They would all now go through intensive interrogation at Palace Barracks, and then be interned.

As his convoy was being driven through the gates of the barracks, the senior British officer in charge of his arrest adopted a friendly tone and said: 'I want to advise you that you should tell everything you know.' The implication was obvious and for the detained 23-year-old man it was hard to decide if the advice was being offered out of sympathy or was just the first of the many onslaughts he expected to suffer in the attempt to break him down. He had decided that no matter what they did to him, he would tell them nothing. They would interrogate him there for 48 hours before interning him but he would tell them nothing, not even his name.

He was brought into a large room in one of the buildings in the barrack compound, where men were sitting around the walls in open booths, some moaning, some showing signs of having been beaten. They brought him to a booth and, like the others, put him sitting with his back to the room, facing the wall. The partitions were a number of feet off the ground and came up to a height of five feet or so. There were about twenty prisoners in the room, all facing the wall, and he could hear the soldiers and policemen coming and going with the men they were bringing off for interrogation. Now and then something frightening would happen behind his back, like a screaming, maniacal policeman coming in, threatening to shoot them all, or sudden loud noises just behind him, such as dropped metal trays or clapping hands.

After some time they came and took him off for interrogation. He was brought to a small room where he was put facing a wall covered with hardboard with numerous perforations. He was put standing spread-eagled just out from the wall, leaning forward with his arms stretched out over his head and his fingers resting on the wall. They beat him until he collapsed and then revived him by throwing water over him. He refused their demand that he resume his spread-eagled position and they beat him again, forcing him to stand up against the wall. He was beaten again and again. Slapped, punched, kicked. But he refused to confirm that he was Gerry Adams. They left him standing against the wall, or sitting staring at it, and the perforations began to assume bizarre images as if he had been drugged. At times they brought him back to the large room and put him sitting facing the wall in a booth. All the time there was shouting, threats, exhibitions of lunacy, the displaying of batons and guns. He was told they had administered a truth drug. He was not allowed sleep.

At one stage during the interrogation, an RUC officer went completely berserk and tried to get out his firearm. His colleagues wrestled with him, but he eventually managed to take out his gun, point it and pull the trigger. The hammer clicked but there was no report. The gun was not loaded. A Special Branch officer long known to republicans in West Belfast, who knew Adams, tried to build up some sort of rapport with him, but his efforts were rejected. The officer changed tactics and threatened to take Adams out with them in RUC cars and have him sitting in the back seat as they carried out a series of raids, knowing full well it could possibly lead to an IRA death sentence against Adams. Still he refused to co-operate. He was brought to another building to have his finger-prints taken, but when he put out his hands to have the fingertips pushed down on the paper, a man appeared wearing a bloodied apron and holding a raised, bloodied hatchet. The man screamed, Adams braced himself wide-eyed and speechless with shock, and then the man disappeared as quickly as he had come.

For Adams, the timing of his arrest was fortunate. Two months earlier, on 30 January 1972, thirteen unarmed people had been shot dead by the British army when they opened fire on people taking part in a banned civil rights march. In the middle of February, seven people had been killed in a bombing in Aldershot, Hampshire, the work of the Official IRA, and on 4 March an enormous PIRA explosion at the Abercorn Bar and Restaurant in Belfast had killed two women and injured 136 people, many of them horribly mutilated. The six counties were erupting and the Northern Ireland parliament at Stormont seemed unable to handle the crisis. There was speculation that London was going to take direct control and that the fall of Stormont was imminent. The interrogators at Palace Barracks, about whom there had been a public outcry because of the flood of harrowing stories emanating from there, were easing off a little in case their new political masters would not condone their actions in the way their current leadership did.

When he was taken from Palace Barracks after 48 hours, Adams was sore, cut and bruised. After 36 hours or so he had admitted his identity, after being told that he was going to be released and then re-arrested and charged with some concocted offence. Not wanting to be locked up under a false name he gave his correct name, but they never did bring him out to charge him. They kept him there, and continued to question and beat him. 'I'm sorry, I can't help you,' he answered repeatedly to their questioning. Nearing the end they grew exasperated with him and let him be. 'I told these fellows that there is no point in talking to you, you've been around too long,' said the RUC officer who had known him since the mid-1960s. 'Well, there you go.... we'll have the whole thing rapped up within six months.'

Before leaving, Adams decided to make a formal complaint that he had been beaten during questioning. It was an unusual request, but he was allowed approach a military policeman sitting behind a desk and tell him what he wanted to do. The soldier called for two military policemen, large intimidating figures, who arrived and wielded batons threateningly; then he asked Adams again and again if he was sure he wanted to make a complaint. After about an hour of this, a uniformed RUC officer was eventually summoned and Adams was allowed to make his formal complaint. Nothing more was ever heard of it.

Prison Ship

They took him to the *Maidstone*, an old British navy vessel moored
in the docks in East Belfast – a Protestant section of the divided city.
There were some 140 men being held on the prison ship, all in
cramped conditions below deck. The bunks were three high,
although Adams (an inch or so over six feet tall) could touch the
ceiling with his hands when standing on the floor. There was little
natural light, save that which came through the portholes. They
were brought up on deck for exercise only occasionally and even
then the high fences which surrounded the deck precluded all but
a small patch of sky. The food was terrible. The sewage from the
prisoners and their guards was simply thrown into the water, and
the stench was enormous. Some time earlier there had been a
celebrated escape – seven republicans had managed to get over the
side of the ship and swim to the shore and freedom. Security was
now so tight that there was no real prospect of the feat being
repeated. For Adams, it seemed the cramped, disgusting conditions on board the *Maidstone* were to be home for quite some time
as, now that they knew who he was, there was little prospect of his
being released until the conflict ended, or until he was too old to
play an active part.

Among the prisoners horror stories of events at Palace Barracks
did the rounds and men showed their wounds to each other as they
told their tales. One had a large, purple circular area around his
navel, caused by his being put hanging by his thumbs so that his
toes just barely touched the ground and his stomach, which was
pulled taut, was then prodded gently again and again and again,
until all the blood-vessels burst. There were tales of people hallu-
cinating, the result of staring at the perforated hardboard walls, of
having genitals squeezed and kicked, of truth drugs and of torture
with 'white noise'.

The ship's gangplank went down onto the dock where an area
was completely enclosed by barbed wire. There were passageways
to small huts, where visits took place. When new arrivals came, the
inmates would crowd up at the portholes, anxious to see who it was
and to deliver shouts and good-humoured jeers. One day a few
army jeeps entered the barbed-wired compound and stopped; the
soldiers took out a young prisoner with a hood over his head. When
the hood was taken off the youth dashed off wildly, screaming all
the time. He came running up against the barbed wire, then turned,

ran in another direction only to bang into the wire again, then turned to run in another direction, all the time screaming. Later it emerged that the soldiers had told him they were going to shoot him, but would give him a chance to run first.

Tension was high on board the *Maidstone*. The soldiers would make occasional searches and were often rough when doing so. There was one particularly bad fight between the soldiers and the prisoners soon after Adams arrived, in which one prisoner had an arm broken. The fight developed into a stand-off between the two sides, and was eventually talked down, with the soldiers having to give up their search in order to avoid an all-out confrontation.

The tension was added to by the prisoners' fear of an attack from the loyalists in surrounding East Belfast in the passionate aftermath of the suspension of the Northern Ireland parliament at Stormont on 24 March 1972, and the introduction of direct rule from London. They were not at all sure that the British army would do its utmost to defend them.

Escape was contemplated, but considered highly unlikely. Adams and a few others developed the idea of going on a solid-food strike in an attempt to attract attention to conditions on the ship. A mass strike was organised, with both the Provisional and the Official IRA prisoners taking part. The relatives outside were organised in support of the campaign and notices from families supporting their menfolk's protest began to appear in the Belfast newspaper, *The Irish News*. The timing was good since it was during the transition period when control was being passed to London. The strike developed into a major issue and on 7 April William Whitelaw, the first holder of the newly created office of Secretary of State for Northern Ireland, announced the closure of the *Maidstone* and the removal by helicopter of the men on board to the prison camp at Long Kesh, near Lisburn.

The Abercorn Bar and Restaurant

Adams was 23 years old. He was one of a small group of Belfast republicans who had warned of the need to be armed and prepared for the violence he was sure was coming as a result of the civil rights movement. When that violence came, he was involved in the defence of his area against the attacks by loyalist crowds and in the fighting with the security forces. The initial welcome which had been proffered by the nationalist community to the British troops on their arrival in Belfast had long been turned to one of resentment and hatred. The small band of republicans who had grouped to form the embryo of the Provos had set up an international arms supply network and were sufficiently well supplied and organised to be able to mount a deadly campaign against what they saw as the occupying army. Moreover there had been a significant increase in recruits following the introduction of internment by Brian Faulkner on 9 August 1971.

By early 1972 the nationalist population hated the British army's presence sufficiently to be able to stomach a campaign of slaughter by the Provos. The scale of violence rose at a horrific rate and the six counties were plunged into a state of war. In 1970, twenty-five people had died in the conflict; in 1971 this figure jumped to 174. Of these, forty-three were British soldiers, five members of the Ulster Defence Regiment (UDR), founded the year before to replace the hated B Specials, and 115 were civilians, including paramilitaries. (Nineteen of the paramilitary casualties were members of the IRA.) By the end of 1972, the worst-ever year for violent deaths in Northern Ireland, 467 people had been killed. Of this horrifically high number, 321 were civilians (with paramilitaries being included in this figure). The IRA had lost sixty-nine members in the violence, and the British troops 103. The UDR lost twenty-six and the RUC lost seventeen members.

A particularly horrific bombing took place on 4 March 1972 in Belfast, the work of members of the 1st Battalion of the PIRA. The bomb exploded at 4.30pm in the Abercorn bar and restaurant which was crowded with tired women and children resting from their shopping. Two women died and 136 people were injured, including two sisters who had been out shopping for a wedding dress and who both had their legs blown off. The horror of the incident and the injuries and mutilations suffered sickened everyone and the movement to end the violence increased. Six days after the explosion, the Provisionals announced a 72-hour cease-fire, as a gesture of good faith and an indication of the level of discipline they could achieve.

However, days later the hostilities resumed. On 20 March a car bomb in Donegall Street in Belfast killed six people and injured 146. Because of atrocities such as these, the PIRA feared a swing against the scale of the killing being carried out. They were anxious to use the position they considered they had won for themselves, before it was taken from them again. A public offer by the Provisionals of a cease-fire if William Whitelaw would meet with them was publicly rejected. However, John Hume and Paddy Devlin of the moderate nationalist Social Democratic and Labour Party (SDLP) met with leading Provisionals Seán MacStiofáin and Daithí Ó Connaill the next day and were given the IRA's conditions for truce talks. Republican prisoners would have to be given political status – leading republican Billy McKee was at the time on hunger-strike in pursuit of political status in the Crumlin Road Prison in Belfast, a potentially explosive situation. An independent witness who was not a politician would have to be present at any truce talks. They could not take place at Stormont, there would be no restrictions on the team which the PIRA could nominate, and Gerry Adams would have to be released to take part in the talks. It was Chief of Staff Seán MacStiofáin's high regard for Adams which led to the demand for his release. When Hume and Devlin put the proposals for the secret talks to Whitelaw, he responded positively.

Call to the Gate

For the inmates of the *Maidstone*, the success of their solid-food strike was a major boost. They were ferried by helicopter from the hated ship to the vastly preferable camp at Long Kesh, later to be renamed 'The Maze'. The prisoners were handcuffed and brought in pairs through a gauntlet of soldiers to a waiting helicopter on the quayside. They considered the gauntlet an attempt at mass intimi-dation at a time when British army fatalities from IRA violence were running high. Adams was one of the last to be taken from the ship, his manacled colleague quite unhappy about who he had had the bad luck to be paired with. But despite the threat, no one was hit during the transfer.

The opening of Long Kesh was evidence that internment was more than a mere trawling exercise and a policy that was at least for the foreseeable future there to stay. It was a clumsy device, and was virtually exclusively targeted at the Catholic working class com-munity. Traditionally the Catholic community unanimously as-pired to a 32-county Republic. Their only difference of opinion was on how it should be achieved. There were nationalists who fa-voured a negotiated settlement through constitutional channels. Republicans on the other hand recognised the legitimacy of waging an armed campaign against the British presence to achieve a united Ireland. Many of those interned were not members of the IRA, though the use of internment without trial undoubtedly meant that many people who otherwise would have taken a different course joined the IRA. But there were other internees who were not in the IRA and did not subsequently become members. Consequently the mere fact that a person was interned was not indicative of IRA membership. At the very most it might mean that they were sympathetic to the IRA's use of force. Similarly the naming of individuals in Long Kesh or elsewhere in this book should not be taken to imply IRA membership. Save in instances where the text makes clear that a named person is an IRA member no such suggestion is made or intended.

Long Kesh was heaven in comparison to the prison ship. There was space, natural light, a relaxed atmosphere, clean air, no unpleasant smell. The camp was organised in 'cages', with a number of huts in each cage, and each cage surrounded by fencing. Each hut and cage had someone in charge, and there was a council in charge of the whole camp. Negotiations between the prisoners and the prison authorities were through appointed 'Officers Commanding' and other camp-appointed prisoners' representatives. All the men from the *Maidstone* were put in the same cage, and such were their feelings of euphoria with the improved conditions they had won, that their antics soon brought them to the disapproving attention of both the camp authorities and their own camp leadership.

One day the British army was put on standby in case troops might be needed to quell a boisterous water-fight that showed no sign of ending. Senior republican Liam Hannaway, an uncle of Adams, remonstrated with the young rowdies and eventually moved into the cage to put a stop to the carry-on.

At one stage, Adams' father, Paddy, his brother Liam, and two of his cousins, as well as his uncle Liam Hannaway, were all in the camp. For the closely knit republican community in West Belfast this was not unusual. The camp had a daily routine and the prisoners appointed people to take charge and make sure the necessary chores were carried out each day. Adams had the task of negotiating with the camp governor on behalf of his cage, something he occasionally did in his underpants or while sitting on the floor on the other side of a table from the governor – all in keeping with the high spirits in the cage and the feelings of defiance.

Nearly all those in the camp were either internees or detainees, 'detainee' being a category that had been introduced by the British to combat the bad publicity that came with the term 'internment'. However, the prisoners in both categories had no release date to give them an indication of what the future held and most suffered from a form of anxiety dubbed 'gate fever' – the constant waiting in the hope of hearing your name called, which could mean going to the gate to be told of your release. Adams, being sure that the British had no intention of releasing him, did not suffer from this condition.

Soon after his arrival in the camp he had however raised the issue of escape, but the general consensus was that escape was impossible and the matter was dropped. There was access to news media and the prisoners were well informed as to what was happening outside. The approaches being made to the British to discuss a cease-fire were secret, but most inmates had an inkling that something was afoot.

Adams and a number of the other more enthusiastic prisoners suggested going on hunger-strike in solidarity with the men in Crumlin Road Prison, and despite the objections of the older men such as Liam Hannaway, who argued that such a strike would be hard to maintain, it went ahead. Adams joined the strike but after fourteen days gave in, unable to carry on – the next day the demand for political status was met and the strike ended.

Adams' uncle, Liam Hannaway, who had been against the hunger-strike, had however joined in and stuck with it, and it is thought that the subsequent damage he did to his health led to his early death.

The day after Adams ended his hunger-strike he was told to go to the gate, that he was being released. It was a common enough ruse to play on prisoners, since the call for those being released could come at any time of the day and releases came in fits and starts, leading to most prisoners being constantly on edge. Adams, convinced that the British were not going to release him, told the prisoner who had passed the message to 'catch himself on'. However, the prisoner persisted and eventually convinced Adams to go to the gate, where to his great surprise he found that he was indeed about to be set free.

The news threw him into some confusion. He worried that he was being released so he could be shot when outside, but his uncle told him to go and he did. Out in the car park he was met by one of the Price sisters (who a year later were to be involved in bombings in the centre of London which killed one and injured 180). He was brought to Andersonstown in West Belfast and told that his release was related to negotiations for a truce and talks with the Secretary of State. The details of the deal being worked out with the British were explained to him.

Adams had paid a brief visit to his parents' home, where he met with his wife Colette, whom he had married ten months earlier. Someone had told her that Adams had been spotted in the Long

Kesh car park and she had made her way to the Adams' home where she found to her amazement that it was true. Within minutes of meeting with his wife Adams had to leave again. All he could tell her was that he was off and he couldn't say where to. He had been told about the demand for the introduction of political status for prisoners and that this would open the way to preliminary talks with British officials, which would in turn prepare the way for talks with Secretary of State Whitelaw. He was taken to Derry by a nationalist politician who was furnished with a pass that would get them safely through any army check-points. Once there he was told that he and Daithí Ó Connaill were to meet with British officials the next day to discuss the introduction of political status, conditions for a truce and the timetable for talks with Whitelaw.

London Talks

The meeting between the two men and the British Government representatives took place in a large country house outside Derry on 20 June 1972, with a solicitor introducing Adams and Ó Connaill to the two British officials, Philip Woodfield and Frank Steele.[2] The issues of political status and conditions for a truce were quickly worked out; the only contention during the straightforward meeting was the timetable for talks with Whitelaw. The British wanted the meeting to take place after the truce had been in existence for fourteen days, while the Irish wanted a meeting seven days after the beginning of the truce. In the end, it was agreed that the meeting would take place after the truce had survived ten days. Before the meeting broke up, the British asked that the Irish remember to make safe any booby traps or land-mines they had set.

Ó Connaill telephoned the IRA's Chief of Staff Seán MacStiofáin, and they made an arrangement to meet and discuss the outcome of the preliminary talks. MacStiofáin suggested to Adams that he go and see his wife for a few days, since the truce would give them all breathing space. Before they parted, Adams told Ó Connaill that he thought the truce was a mistake, that he did not believe the British were ready to leave or that there was any other strategy which could be developed through the truce.

Adams made his way back to Belfast where he spent the next ten days at home with his wife and parents. He had married Colette while on the run following the introduction of internment, so this was the first time they could be together without worrying about arrest. He often met with fellow republicans during this quiet time, to explain to them the terms of the truce. However, it was not a totally peaceful period. One night the Adams' family were woken at around 2am by a blast of shooting – the RUC had shot dead a man who had driven through a road-block just down the road from their home. On another occasion a major stand-off developed in Bally-murphy, where a group of up to sixty IRA men, armed with everything from pickaxes to Thompson machine guns, were stand-ing down the road from a band of British soldiers, refusing to let them enter Ballymurphy. The IRA contingent was led by a man who had escaped from prison and the British army officer took exception to such a person telling him what to do. (The truce terms included a withdrawal of troops from such sensitive areas.) Eventually a phone call from Adams to a contact on the British side led to the troops being told to withdraw.

At 8am on the morning of Friday 7 July the republican Sinn Féin team – comprising Seán MacStiofáin, Daithí Ó Connaill, Belfast republicans Seamus Twomey and Ivor Bell, Derry republican Martin McGuinness (who like Adams was in his early twenties) and Adams – left in two cars from Derry for their rendezvous with the British. On the way one of the cars broke down, so the six crowded into the small second car along with their driver. When they met up with the British army team they were put in a minibus, its windows covered with brown paper, and brought to a field, where an army helicopter was waiting to fly them to Aldergrove airport outside Belfast. Of the republican team, MacStiofáin and at least one other member of the group were armed, MacStiofáin carrying a .38 Cobra special revolver in a shoulder holster.[3] It was a glorious morning and the republicans admired the landscape of Northern Ireland as the British army helicopter flew them towards Belfast.

On landing at Aldergrove they were quickly transferred to an RAF plane which took them to Benson RAF station in Oxfordshire. Two limousines were waiting to take the group to London, with the cars making one stop on the way, in a small village, so that Seamus Twomey could go to the toilet and also buy cigarettes. It being a nice day, Twomey took his time walking around the pleasant setting searching for cigarettes for Adams. His twenty-minute absence almost caused heart failure to the members of the British escort travelling with the strange convoy.

The group were brought to a house at Cheyne Walk in Chelsea, on the banks of the Thames, the home of Paul Channon, a relation of the Guinness family, and a junior minister to Whitelaw who was later to be a minister in the Thatcher government. The Irish group had already decided what they wanted from the British was a declaration of intent to withdraw from Northern Ireland. When Whitelaw arrived, MacStiofáin outlined their demands, which included a withdrawal from sensitive areas pending a complete withdrawal in less than three years, that is by January 1975. During the meeting there were a number of emotional outbursts, with one of the most dramatic coming from McGuinness who angrily brought up the subject of 'Bloody Sunday', when the British army had shot dead thirteen unarmed people in Derry, after Whitelaw had said the British army would never open fire on unarmed civilians.

Whitelaw agreed to put the Irish demands to the Cabinet on condition that the truce remained in effect. The sticking point which developed between the two sides was how long this might take, with Whitelaw pushing for longer than the Irishmen were prepared to accept. In the end it was agreed that the Cabinet reply would be given in one week. There was also discussion about the release of internees, with the British trying to link the rate of releases to the honouring of the truce, and the Irish arguing that the internees should be released as a matter of right. During the whole day, Adams (who like his friend Ivor Bell had dressed scruffily for the historic meeting) remained quiet. He did, however, during a ten minute adjournment express disquiet about the amount of time being given to the British to return with their reply. At another stage, Whitelaw had said the talks were secret and that if they became public, then 'all bets are off'. Adams took exception to what he considered the arrogance of the remark – which was later to be repeated to him in very different circumstances – and he testily echoed Whitelaw's remark back to him: 'Yes, all bets are off.'

On the return flight in the RAF plane, the Irish negotiating team were served a meal, during which a British official said to Twomey and MacStiofáin: 'I hope you are not going to start your bloody stupid campaign again.' MacStiofáin got the distinct impression that the official was not unduly worried about the scale of the carnage in Northern Ireland, with British casualties there being, as the official said, roughly equal to those suffered by the army from traffic accidents in West Germany.[4] Adams, who still did not see any prospect of success from the London talks, sang 'The Belfast Brigade' with Ivor Bell as they winged their way home.

Adams believed that the British had organised the truce and the talks for a number of reasons. Firstly, as a fact-finding exercise, so they could identify and meet the top republicans. Secondly, because they wanted to see if what was essentially a state of insurgency in Northern Ireland, with about one security force casualty per day, could be ended. And finally, because they had been advised by the military that if a guerrilla army can be stood down for a period it is difficult for it to get back into action again. With a regular army, when a conflict ends the troops simply retire to their barracks, to train and parade, and remain ready for any further conflict. But with a guerrilla group like the IRA, when the conflict ends, most of the force return to everyday life and leave the organisation. If the conflict then erupts again, many will be slow to return and the organisation will have been weakened.

Nevertheless, the British now faced the problem of how to end the truce because a British rejection of the Irish 'peace proposals', Adams believed, could be used along with the existence of internment, as propaganda by the republicans.

MacStiofáin was anxious that the truce hold for as long as possible since, he thought, it might allow the holding of a conference of Irish groups of all political and religious denominations to discuss the North. In order to get the Protestant groups to take part in any such talks, it would be necessary for the truce to hold, so that sectarian tensions could ease. He believed that if progress could be made towards such a conference, it would put pressure on the British not to reject the Irish demands completely.

However, since the start of the truce there had been a heightening of sectarian tension. In the five days between June 30 and July 4, there were nine seemingly tit for tat sectarian killings. Four Protestants, four Catholics, and a Jehovah's Witness were killed. In almost all cases the victims were abducted and later, with bullets shot into their heads, they were dumped onto the side of the road. In the Rathcoole area of Belfast, all 300 Catholic families had to flee their homes in fear of their lives. When it was decided to move them into houses earlier vacated by Protestants in the Lenadoon area, the loyalist paramilitary group the Ulster Defence Association (UDA) threatened to burn them out. On the Sunday following the truce talks, the British army turned back a furniture van bringing the belongings of a Catholic family to their allocated house in Lenadoon, because of the UDA threats. A confrontation followed during which CS gas was fired at the Catholic crowd which had gathered. The local Provisional leader decided the terms of the truce had been broken and the IRA opened fire on the soldiers. At 7pm on the Sunday following the London talks, MacStiofáin made the official announcement that the truce was over.

Adams had been involved during the truce in defusing tense situations in Belfast, but he had not been contacted before the issue in Lenadoon descended into conflict. He was astonished when a colleague came to him and told him of the ending of the truce. Annoyed that he had not been warned earlier, he quickly left the house where he was and met up with some colleagues preparing for 'active service'. From now on he could no longer remain at his parents' home where he had been staying with his wife. Within two days the house was raided by the army. He was back on the run.

2: Falls Memories

West Belfast, a drab network of terraced working-class housing, is home for the majority of the Catholics living in the capital of Northern Ireland. In the turbulent years before and after the winning of independence for twenty-six of Ireland's thirty-two counties, the minority Catholic population in Belfast had been under siege from the majority Protestant one. The sectarian violence eventually all but disappeared but the fear remained. The Catholic working-class population resigned themselves to a life of discrimination and disadvantage, in a statelet where the leaders of the ruling Unionist Party made little effort to conceal the importance they gave to ensuring continuing Protestant dominance. For the entire Catholic population of the six counties, but especially for the outnumbered residents in West Belfast who lived so close to similar Protestant areas, fear lay at the bottom of their political relationship with the state.

The Pound Looney was a particularly intimate network of working-class housing which lay off the Falls Road in the Ballymurphy area and it was here on Leeson Street that Gerry Adams was born on 6 October 1948. Both his father Paddy and his mother Anne were republicans. Paddy had been shot by the RUC in his youth, was a member of the IRA and had been imprisoned in the 1940s. His mother was a member of the Hannaway family, a well-respected, if not legendary, family among Belfast republicans. Adams' maternal grandfather had known the Irish socialist and revolutionary James Connolly and the forceful trade unionist Jim Larkin; he had campaigned for de Valera during the 1918 Irish elections, after which Sinn Féin set up a Provisional Government, the first Dáil. His paternal grandfather and in-laws were involved in the IRA.

Adams was one of ten children (there were thirteen births but one set of twins and another infant died soon after being born) and the family were by no means prosperous. At one stage, in 1961, having just returned from England where he had been working, Paddy Adams gave serious consideration to taking his family to Australia.

Adams went to the local primary and secondary schools run by the Christian Brothers, St Finian's and St Mary's, briefly attending

St Gabriel's in between. As a student he showed an above average ability, worked hard at his studies, won an 11-plus scholarship and performed well enough in his O levels for the scholarship to be extended, to allow him study for his A levels. He was interested in the Irish language and history, and had arguments in school over the fact that they were being taught English rather than Irish history. He was an enthusiastic, though not a greatly skilled, sportsman; he played for his school hurling teams, as well as taking part in cross-country running and just about any form of athletics going. He joined a boxing club on the Shankill Road, but left it after a few weeks.

Life in the Pound Looney was an intimate if isolated one for a young boy, whose early years were spent happily unaware of the nature of the state in which he lived and what it meant for a working-class Catholic, as Adams himself recalls:[1].

> In Divis Street a woman sold us hot home-made soda farls and pancakes plastered with jam. Brother Beausang packed us into the Ard Schoil for the oral exams to win a place in the Donegal Gaeltacht; Ducky Mallon taught us our sevens; and lunch breaks were spent playing football beside the glass factory and afterwards seeing who could pee the highest in the school bog. Handball at the gable walls in St Mary's, or cards and cigarettes for the big lads were the lunch-time diversions...
>
> We were all part of a new generation of working-class Taigs [Catholics], winning scholarships to grammar schools and 'getting chances' which as our parents and grandparents frequently reminded us, they never had. We wore school uniforms – a fairly new and expensive luxury – and were slightly bemused to see our mirror reflections in Austin's, the school outfitters, just below Dover Street...
>
> Summer evenings were spent in the Falls Park playing hurling and football with infrequent formal handball sessions at handball alleys at St Malachy's. During the winter we cadged money for the Clonard, Broadway or Diamond picture houses, or for the baths and, exams to one side, life was pleasant and uneventful.

However sectarianism soon made its ugly presence known. For Adams it was when a number of bullies stopped him and told him to recite a Catholic prayer; he started to cry. The children of West Belfast gradually became aware of the ugly nature of the town and state where they had been born. They made decisions on how to deal with their predicament, some opting to leave, some deciding to stay. Adams saw that there were three options for a Catholic youth; to emigrate, to stay and adopt an attitude of passivity, or to stay and try to change the nature of the state. He decided to stay and fight.

The Paisley Riots

In 1963, on the 200th anniversary of the death of Wolfe Tone, the adopted founding father of Irish republicanism, the republican movement established Wolfe Tone committees throughout Ireland. These were to act as a forum for progressive and anti-imperialistic political ideas and as a meeting place for socialists, republicans and Irish-language enthusiasts. The movement was delivered a major boost three years after its formation, with the 50th anniversary of the 1916 Easter Rising in 1966.

In the 1964 British general election, the Sinn Féin and IRA member Liam McMillen stood for election in West Belfast on the republican ticket. During the campaign an Irish tricolour was displayed in a window of the Sinn Féin offices on Divis Street off the Falls Road. The display was not illegal, but could be banned under the Flags and Emblems Act if its display was likely to lead to a breach of the peace. The RUC decided that it was best to ignore the flag's display on the Falls, but on Sunday, 27 September, the staunch loyalist, the Reverend Ian Paisley, threatened at an Ulster Hall rally that if the offending flag was not removed, he would lead a march of his supporters into West Belfast to ensure that it was. The police, conscious that Paisley had the power to cause considerable disturbance, decided the flag should be removed and they took it down the next day. Paisley called off his march and a victorious rally was held outside City Hall instead. Some Catholics had gathered at the Divis Street headquarters expecting Paisley and there were some clashes there with the RUC.

The next night there was more rioting in West Belfast and a number of buses were burned. On Thursday the flag was back in the window. The RUC again decided that it should be removed. Ironically, the constable who was designated with the task was a Catholic. The party of RUC men encountered resistance and had to smash the window with pickaxes to remove the flag. By the evening, rioting had broken out and the RUC were forced to bring in water cannons in their efforts to beat back the crowds. The Catholics threw petrol bombs at the police and the IRA sent out some members armed with hand-guns. The riots were the worst Belfast had seen since the 1930s.

To be a republican in Belfast meant to invite the attention of the RUC's Special Branch and a certain amount of harassment. The Catholic community in times of tension looked to the IRA for protection, but tended to avoid them at other times, since to be seen to be close to them attracted suspicion from the police. During the explosion of republican feeling that surrounded the 50th anniversary celebrations in 1966, to be a Belfast republican became for a time more 'respectable'. The writings of James Connolly and others were promoted and found a new audience and the Republic's television station, RTE, broadcast a reconstruction of the 1916 Rising which made a lasting impression on many Irish people for whom television itself was a new and exciting phenomenon. In Belfast, an Easter Sunday parade was organised and attracted a crowd of 10,000. Seventeen-year-old Gerry Adams got to see himself on television, acting as a steward for the march as it made its way down the Falls Road.

Adams did not see much of the 1964 rioting but while coming and going to school he saw the flag in the Sinn Féin office and later the empty, smashed window after the RUC had taken the tricolour away. The teachers at his school told their students to go straight home, but Adams and a few others would loiter around the Sinn Féin offices on the way. One evening, after the removed tricolour had been replaced, the assembled crowd broke into the Irish national anthem, Amhrán na bhFiann. On the night of fiercest rioting, Adams was in the Felons Club above Hector's shop on Linden Street, a few streets away from Divis Street, folding election literature for Liam McMillen. While he worked in the Club that night, the fighting raged around him, but he did not get involved. However, that incident, he was to say later, led him to start questioning the constitutional status of the land in which he lived. With a family already active in republican politics and frequenting such places as the Felons Club, the Ard Schoil and the '43 Club, where Irish cultural and political activities were organised by republicans, Adams was given a wealth of political information and opinion in reply.

He joined Sinn Féin in 1964 and later Na Fianna, the 'boy scouts' of the republican movement. His political education was leading him to the view that the status of Northern Ireland was that of a colony and that independence and a united Ireland were ideals worth striving, and fighting, for. He thus became a committed member of the republican movement.

The IRA's Belfast Brigade had retained its military structure of battalions and companies, but by the mid-60s there was only a bunch of about sixty men who could, with any truth, call themselves members of the IRA. There was almost no military activity and the emphasis was increasingly moving towards politics.

Adams and his republican colleagues used meet in a small room in Cyprus Street GAA club, where there were lectures and discussions on such subjects as Fenians and Fenianism, colonialism, neo-colonialism, partition and British imperialism.[2] At that time Sinn Féin was an illegal organisation, made up a of a small incestuous group which had few young members. The republican movement, having shed most of its militaristic tendencies, was developing into a small politically conscious organisation. A new politically-minded leadership in Dublin was leading the organisation to the view that there was a need to create a vision relevant to the needs of Ireland in the 1960s and a need to build up as much popular support as possible.

In 1965 the first of the Republican Clubs – centres for social and political activity for republicans – was set up in Belfast in a drive aimed at ending the ban on Sinn Féin. The Adams family had moved to Andersonstown and Gerry Adams joined the Republican Club there. By 1967 he had been appointed its public relations officer. The existence of the Republican Clubs was publicly declared and they too were banned. A campaign began in protest against this which attracted a broad spectrum of political activists. Adams, in a planned defiance of the ban on the sale of the *United Irishman* newspaper, was arrested for selling it in public. However, much to their annoyance, he and a colleague arrested along with him were released after a short time and robbed of the publicity they were seeking.

In the drive to bring their political ideas to the population, agitational and protest committees started up, and Adams was one of the few committed republicans in Belfast who threw himself enthusiastically into this work.

Apprentice Barman

On a whim one day during school lunch-break early in 1966, Gerry Adams walked across the Protestant Shankill Road and into the Ark Bar on the Old Lodge Road. He asked for a job as a barman and was told he could start on Monday. That evening when he went home and announced the news, his father, who had been hoping his son would sit his A levels and possibly go on to university, was annoyed. But Adams had felt the peer-group pressure from his friends, who were all leaving school, getting their first jobs and earning their first pay-packets, and he had succumbed.

The customers in the bar were mostly working-class Protestants, with a sprinkling of Catholics. There was plenty of 'crack' and politics was rarely discussed. Some of the customers would occasionally say that if the Catholics would only keep quiet, then everything would be all right. On the evening of 17 March, the special day for the patron saint of Ireland, St Patrick, a number of Protestant customers sang the republican ballad 'Kevin Barry' for Adams and he in turn gave a rendition of the loyalist song 'The Sash'.

As the important loyalist day of 12 July approached, however, so too did a noticeable sectarian tension.

The job was not to last long. The barmen's union had an agreement with the Vintners Association that in return for working the 'glorious 12th', the workers would be paid a double day's pay and a day off in lieu. When 12 July came, Adams asked for what had been agreed but was refused by the bar's owner, a Catholic, as most publicans were in Belfast at the time. Adams took his case to the union, which he considered should support him in his fight for the agreed terms. The trade union, however, was reluctant to support the angry young bar apprentice and, after having a fight with them and his boss, Adams found himself without a job. The irony of the incident was not lost on the bar's customers who, in a gesture of goodwill, raised a collection for him as a parting gift.

Adams had the satisfaction of leaving his employer on one of the busiest nights of the year for the pub, to go strolling up the Shankill Road taking in the atmosphere of the loyalist festival, with its bonfires, drinking and singing of sectarian songs.

He quickly got another job, this time in the Duke of York, a city-centre pub frequented by a colourful crowd of trade unionists, journalists, communists and members of the Northern Ireland Labour Party, as well as unionist politicians, judges, and employees of the Director of Public Prosecutions office. It was a fascinating place for a young man interested in politics and he kept the job there until the events of the summer of 1969 left him with no time for anything except street-fighting.

Civil Rights

Adams reacted enthusiastically to Liam McMillen's call to republicans to get involved in the campaign opposing the planned building of the high-rise housing complex in West Belfast, the Divis Flats. Republicans claimed they were going to make for cheap, unsatisfactory homes, as had been the experience with such schemes in other countries. Adams visited Derry and Dublin and saw how the housing action committees there were organising their campaigns. Along with a number of others he set up the West Belfast Housing Action Committee and began to spend an increasing amount of his free time attending meetings, writing letters and organising protest squats in the ongoing battle for better housing.

The first major venture of the West Belfast Housing Action Committee involved a family, the Sherlocks, who lived in a two-bedroomed house on Mary Street just off the Falls Road. The Sherlock's home was in bad condition (as were many of the houses on Mary Street) and Adams and his colleagues brought the family to the Housing Trust to try and have them allocated a better house. When that proved unsuccessful, they took over a flat in what was the beginning of the Divis Flats complex. Being the first such incident in Belfast, it attracted considerable media attention and eventually proved successful, with the Sherlocks being allocated a new home.

The experience was both encouraging and educational, proving that direct action could get results and enjoy popular support. The group began a campaign of occupations and picketing of the Housing Trust's offices and soon found that people were coming to them looking for help with their housing problems. Adams took note of how they had managed to win popular support in the Sherlock fight – in contrast to their lack of support in the earlier, unsuccessful, campaign against the Divis Flats. He now sought for ways to use the same methods in his agitational work against unemployment. In addition, when the Northern Ireland Civil Rights Association (NICRA) was being formed, he was a founding member.

He and his colleagues fitted easily into the campaign. Northern Ireland in the early 1960s was a one-party state, ruled by the Protestant Unionist Party who controlled a territory where the drawing of political boundaries, access to a vote and discrimination in housing and employment were all used to ensure a continuing Protestant majority. This they saw as a bulwark against unification with the Irish Republic, which they saw, with much justification, as a Catholic, 'Rome-ruled' state where their traditions and beliefs would be destroyed.

After the winning of independence for the twenty-six counties in 1922, the remaining six north-eastern counties had suffered horrific sectarian violence, but it had eventually subsided and by the 1960s it looked as if the Northern Irish state was firmly established. However, the granting of free education by the British government led to the growth of an educated Catholic youth in Northern Ireland during the 1960s, who were less willing than their parents to accept their lot as second-class citizens. They began to press for what they saw as their rightful place in the state that was their home. Their campaign gathered momentum in a decade in which a wave of hopeful political agitation seemed to be changing the world for the better. In the USA, there was a campaign for civil rights for black people; there were anti-nuclear and anti-war protests, and popular songwriters sang songs of love and brotherhood. Political change was being sung about on records, television, even in the bars and halls of Belfast. It was hard to doubt that the evils of Northern Ireland could not also be changed.

In 1963 Con and Patricia McCloskey from Dungannon, Co. Tyrone, had organised the Catholic women of their town to protest outside the council offices against discrimination in housing allocation. They began to build up a dossier of other examples of unionist bias in council employment, calling their project the Campaign for Social Justice. What they had planted was the seed from which was to grow the civil rights movement in Northern Ireland.

NICRA marches

For many of the volunteers in the IRA's Belfast Brigade, the growing emphasis on politics and the playing down of the military aspect of the IRA were anathema. As a result, they drifted away from the movement.

Adams, while he was enthusiastically involved in the political work being advocated by the leadership of the republican movement in Dublin and by McMillen in Belfast, believed that the leadership's theories were flawed. It believed that in order to allow the push for full civil rights to develop in the six counties – so that a social and economic campaign involving the Catholic and Protestant working-class could develop and, in turn, a united republican working-class – the national question should be subordinated. Adams felt that this underestimated the reactionary nature of the Northern Ireland state and the resistance of the Westminster and Stormont rulers to reform. He felt that the civil rights question would rapidly turn into the national question and that the situation in the six counties could quickly become more dangerous than the Dublin leadership realised. He believed that the Northern Ireland state was by its very nature unreformable and that the forces released by the civil rights movement were set on a collision course with this fact. The Dublin leadership visited Belfast to lecture on their idea of the 'stages theory', of how the united democratic republic would come about. Adams attended these lectures and found the theorising interesting but always felt it did not fit in with his experience of life in Northern Ireland. The theories were divorced from reality.

Even the minor attempts at cross-community political and agitational involvement he had witnessed had foundered on the rock of sectarianism. His neighbourhood of Catholic Ballymurphy enjoyed good relations with the neighbouring Protestant Moynard and New Barnseley estates. When a child from New Barnseley was knocked down on the Springfield Road, Adams went to the estate and spoke with the parents of the child and then went back to the well-organised residents association in Ballymurphy. A small campaign for safety railings and a pedestrian crossing for the dangerous part of the road was begun. The campaign was successful, to the delight of all concerned. But when news of the this cross-community co-operation spread, supporters of the Reverend Ian Paisley visited the area and talk of 'papists, pope-heads and fenians' was suddenly being heard.[3] There was a rise in sectarian tension and the residents of New Barnseley quickly ended their involvement with the Catholics of Ballymurphy. Adams believed that the 'playing of the sectarian card' would always put an end to any progress made along the lines being advocated by the Dublin leadership.

Meanwhile, the civil rights struggle was gathering momentum and the first Northern Ireland Civil Rights Association (NICRA) march took place from Coalisland to Dungannon in August 1968. Later that year, in October, when a planned march for Derry was banned by Stormont, the marchers decided to go ahead with their plans anyway. However, the RUC put a police cordon across their route and when the marchers came to it the police, after some discussion with the marchers, suddenly started to hit them with their batons. The crowd panicked and was chased by the police who beat the fleeing marchers mercilessly around the head and body. The nationalist MP for West Belfast, Gerry Fitt, was beaten on the head and pictures of him with blood streaming down his neck were carried by newspapers around the world. The baton charge itself was filmed by TV crews and broadcast internationally to the enormous embarrassment of the British government.

Adams, who had not been able to get the day off work to attend the banned march, watched the TV pictures while standing behind the bar in the Duke of York. For him, the images gave substance to the belief he held – that the demand by Catholics for civil rights was in essence a demand for the dismantling of the Northern Ireland state.

3: The North Erupts

The second largest city in Northern Ireland, Derry, had a majority Catholic population but by skilful drawing of boundaries and allocation of houses, it had been ruled politically by the unionists since partition in 1922. Tension had been mounting in the city in the early months of 1969, with stone-throwing and small-scale riots becoming increasingly common. A housing action committee had been set up there before the Belfast one and it had been successful in drawing attention to the issues of bad housing and discrimination.

As the 1969 loyalist marching season of July and August approached, the Catholics in Derry's working-class estates discussed the issue of defending their communities. These marches had always made for increased sectarian tensions in the six counties, being a time when the ruling loyalist tradition indulged in a celebration which often included strong elements of triumphalism, a sort of symbolic pageant illustrating the state and nature of the relationship between the two communities. The Catholic population through the years had suffered the taunts of the season quietly, but now, with heightened tension and mounting feelings of defiance among the nationalists, a head-on collision looked inevitable.

Within the IRA nationally, the issue as to what role the movement should take was producing heated discussion. For the leadership, intent on their 'stages theory' and the gradual coming together of the Protestant and Catholic working-classes, the idea of acting as a defence organisation for the Catholic population against the Protestant one was horrifying. A more sectarian role would be hard to imagine. But many northern Catholic republicans, concerned about the safety of their community, decided to ignore the leadership's thinking and began to set up and organise vigilante street committees for their defence.

Derry Erupts

There had been serious rioting during and after the 12 July celebrations in Derry in 1969, and both the security forces and the nationalist population in the Bogside area feared worse for 12 August, the day of the Apprentice Boys' parade, traditionally the bigger of the two occasions in the city. In the Bogside, residents set about organising and erecting barricades, building up stocks of stones to be used as missiles, and bottles to be used in making petrol bombs. The use of firearms was ruled out.

In Belfast, the tension had also been rising steadily during the early months of 1969. Adams found the RUC were reacting in an increasingly violent manner to the protests he and his colleagues were organising around the now-built Divis Flats and in West Belfast generally. The police, during each outbreak of violence, made a direct line for him and his colleagues whenever there was a baton charge, having identified them as the principal agitators. On one occasion at Hastings Street Barracks, where there was frequent rioting, the protesters turned to face the police when they launched their baton charge; the police about-faced and fled back into their barracks. Adams and about fifty others, armed with a telegraph pole, began to ram the door of the barracks in an attempt to break it down. Eventually he and another man were accepted into the station as a delegation, to outline their views to the bewildered RUC.[1]

With riots occurring with increasing frequency, Adams felt the republican leadership was unable to give proper direction and was at a loss as to what to do. He began to have regular arguments with his senior political colleague, Liam McMillen, as his fears grew of the conflict he felt lay ahead and for which he felt they were not prepared. By July, he and his colleagues were organising the defence of the Ardoyne and Unity Flats against expected fresh RUC and loyalist attacks during the forthcoming loyalist marches.

In Derry on 12 August in the early afternoon, 15,000 Apprentice Boys began their loyalist march around the city. The RUC kept a gang of nationalist youths behind barricades as the parade passed Waterloo Place, but as they passed, someone in the crowd threw a handful of nails at the police, and these were quickly followed by bricks and stones. A fierce riot began which was to last two days. During the fighting, the exhausted RUC were given permission to fire CS gas into the crowds in their efforts to control the situation. The Taoiseach, the Prime Minister of the Irish Republic, Jack Lynch, made a speech in which he promised that his government 'would not stand idly by', leading many nationalists to believe that southern troops were about to be sent into the six counties. It was just as the dreaded 'B Specials' were advancing on the Bogside near the end of the second day of fighting that the British army was deployed on the streets of Derry. To the disgust of the republicans, the exhausted and frightened Bogsiders warmly welcomed the soldiers' arrival and, they thought, the coming of peace.

During the riots, the civil rights leaders in Derry appealed to their colleagues throughout the north to stage demonstrations which it was hoped would draw police resources away from Derry, where the RUC had been attacking nationalists and wrecking their homes. NICRA leaders in Belfast were worried about holding any such protests, since they feared the consequences of releasing the sectarian hatred and tension that existed there. An emergency meeting of civil rights activists in Belfast heard a taped impassioned plea from Derry for demonstrations. Adams proposed that a protest be held on the Falls Road in West Belfast, making his proposal on behalf of the West Belfast Housing Action Committee. He argued that there was little difference between looking for better housing for the people of West Belfast and expressing solidarity with the people of the Bogside who were being beaten up for making the same demand. It was agreed to go ahead with a Belfast protest. Adams and his colleagues went off to make petrol bombs.[2]

Belfast Erupts

On 13 August the protesters in Belfast gathered at the Divis Flats and marched to Springfield Road RUC station. It was a peaceful and orderly march, with about 200 taking part. But when the marchers arrived at the station and tried to hand in their petition, they were told that the police headquarters for the area had been moved temporarily to Hastings Street station and that they would have to hand in their protest there. Irritated, the protesters marched back the way they had come, while the officer who had refused to receive their protest made his way to the Hastings Street station to receive the petition.

While the crowd had been waiting at Springfield Road, some had thrown stones at the police station, and a number of windows were broken.

When they arrived back up at Hastings Street, a group of teenagers again began to throw stones, but this time a number of them who lived nearby produced petrol bombs and began to hurl them at the building. The RUC responded with excessive force, deciding to deploy armoured cars, which they had for policing Northern Ireland. The crowd ran away from the armoured cars as they came screeching out of the police courtyard, but some youths soon returned and continued fighting, enraged at the heavy-handed response from the police. This time they were armed with crates of petrol bombs. The police fired on the crowd, injuring two, and some of the nationalists who had guns returned fire. When the police opened fire with automatic weapons over the crowd, it finally dispersed.

A police Humber which drew up at nearby Leeson Street had been hit by the explosion of an American-made grenade and this gave substance to an RUC belief that the IRA were planning to launch a full-scale uprising. It was decided to mount high velocity, heavy .30 calibre Browning machine-guns on their armoured cars. These guns have a range of almost two-and-half miles and fire six to eight high velocity bullets every second. They can only fire bursts, never single shots. The police were to use these lethal weapons in an effort at crowd control in narrow, winding city streets.

Adams was to have been working at the bar of the Duke of York on the night of the rioting, but instead he remained in the Springfield Road area to take part in the fighting. The next day, he made his way to work and apologised for his absence the night before. All summer he had been finding it more and more difficult to fit his work in. In the early afternoon of the day following the rioting, the republican leader in Belfast came to the pub and asked Adams and another republican who worked there if they would come up to the Falls Road to help out. They agreed and left, bringing with them brown paper bags filled with empty Guinness bottles for making petrol bombs. Before he left, Adams' boss told him the job would be there for him when he was ready to come back.

Belfast erupted that night. All around Catholic West Belfast Protestant crowds gathered, building up their stores of rocks and petrol bombs; Catholics erected barricades in the hope of keeping them out. In the evening, a crowd of young Catholic men made their way to Hastings Street RUC station and began to shower it with petrol bombs and whatever stone or metal missiles they could find. A Catholic crowd was making its way along Dover Street protected behind a moving barricade of corrugated iron, driving the Protestant crowd before it. Petrol bombs and missiles were thrown by both sides and houses and local halls went up in flames. When RUC armoured cars arrived and broke through the moving Catholic barricade, the Protestant crowd and the B Specials poured through the gap and the two sides set upon one another, the battleground lit up by the burning buildings on both sides of the street. All over West Belfast similar riots were taking place, floodlit

by blazing buildings. On Cupar Street about 400 Catholics and
Protestants were fighting; the RUC having decided the Catholic
crowd were the greater danger to them, decided to baton
charge them. As the police began their assault, IRA gunmen
opened fire on them – the first acknowledged IRA action in the
current conflict. The crowd and the RUC took cover, and the police
began to return fire. Five people were wounded in the exchange.

On Dover Street, where the rioting had been going on for up to
seven hours, the IRA also opened fire. Fearing that the Protestants
were going to gain a breakthrough, they began to pour fire into the
mouth of the street. Herbert Roy, a 26-year-old Protestant, was
looking around the corner and was hit in the chest by a .38 bullet.
He fell to the ground, dying. Three members of the RUC were also
hit in the shooting, which ended when the RUC sent out three
Shortlands – the heavy-wheeled armoured personnel carriers with
.30 Browning machine-guns mounted, guns capable of shooting
through brick walls. Later, when the police decided they were
being shot at from the Divis Flats, they fired off several bursts in that
direction. One of the bullets passed through the walls of No. 5, St
Brendan's Path, killing nine-year-old Patrick Rooney in his bed.
The young boy was hit in the head by the heavy calibre bullet, his
blood and brains splattered onto his bedroom wall.

West Belfast was turning into a terrifying and surreal war zone.
The RUC were driving around in the Shortlands, occasionally
letting off short bursts of the heavy calibre bullets. They were using
tracers and the horrified people watched as the glowing streams of
deadly lead cut through the air of their neighbourhood. On
numerous streets on the perimeter of the Catholic ghetto, families
were fleeing their homes and heading deeper into the nationalist
area, while Protestants entered the vacated Catholic homes,
wrecking them and setting them ablaze.

Near Divis Street a group of six young IRA men and three non-
members had taken up position in St Comgall's Catholic school in
the hope of preventing the school, and the nearby St Peter's church,
from being burned down. Armed Protestants began to attack them
and they desperately held them off for an hour, using petrol bombs.
They were joined by a group of several well-known, middle-aged
republicans, who were armed with a Thompson sub-machine-gun,
a .303 rifle, four pistols and enough ammunition to allow them to
pour fire down on the streets below for over an hour. The action
came to be seen by the people of West Belfast as having prevented
their suffering from being even worse that night. It was considered

the only time during the fighting that the IRA were seen to have lived up to their role as the defenders of the Belfast Catholics. Disgust with the republican performance in general – a huge number of Catholic homes were burned out during the night – led to graffiti artists daubing walls with slogans such as 'IRA – I ran away'.

Adams later wrote about this period in a republican publication.[3]

> He [Adams] thought of August 14th/15th, only a few months past. Cursed nailbombs without detonators. Bulmer [Adjutant with B. Co., 2nd Batt., Liam McParland, who was to die in a car crash on 6 November] complained a lot about that. An RUC Shortland car drove over one. Nothing happened
>
> A waste of time throwing them at anything which was armed with Browning machine-guns. He remembered the scene that night in Divis Street. He thought of the first time he and Bulmer got together. Bulmer did the driving. They laughed about it afterwards. They had to push the car most of the way. Bulmer didn't drive after that. He volunteered not to. He made up for it in the Murph. Plenty of organising behind barricades. Standbys, lectures, recruiting, meeting people, getting gear, rushing here, there and everywhere. The standbys were good crack. Up Springhill Avenue or behind Corry's sitting 'til daylight swopping stories. Bulmer and the man with the cap talked about the 50s while he himself spoofed about riots, about Civil Rights meetings, and housing or unemployment agitation. He liked the standbys. They discussed what was going to happen and how things would work out. It was good crack then.

At dawn on 15 August, families on the perimeter of Catholic West Belfast left their homes with whatever possessions they could carry and made for safe areas deeper in the Catholic enclave. During the previous night, six people had lost their lives in the sectarian violence. The RUC chiefs and their political masters still believed that the IRA (who in reality had only a handful of firearms) were planning a rebellion. And the Protestants believed that the evacuation of the perimeter housing was in some way in preparation for this rebellion.

At 4.30am, the Commissioner of Police for Belfast had made a request that British soldiers be sent in to relieve his exhausted men. Early that afternoon the request was granted by the British Home Office and that evening – again to the annoyance of republicans – the nationalist population in Belfast were welcoming the arrival of British troops onto their streets.

However, the coming of the troops did not lead to an immediate cessation of hostilities. Errors in the handing over of responsibility from the police to the army allowed rioting to flare in the Clonard district, where a 15-year-old member of Na Fianna, Gerard McCauley, was shot through the heart while helping a Catholic family move from their home. The youth is now honoured by the Provisional IRA as the first volunteer to die in the current conflict. In the Ardoyne during a series of shooting incidents which followed the removal of the police, a Protestant man, David Linton (48) died after he was hit in the face with a shotgun blast.

By the time the fighting ended, on Sunday, 17 August, seven people had been killed and about 750 injured, with at least seventy-two Catholics and sixty-one Protestants suffering gunshot wounds. Of the 1,820 families who fled their homes because of burnings, damage or fear, 1,505 were Catholic and 315 Protestant. It was the biggest refugee movement in Europe since the end of the Second World War.

4: The Birth of the Provisionals

During the 1960s, as the republican movement had become increasingly politicised and moved away from its military tradition, a number of the older veteran republicans had left in distaste. When the violence erupted in August 1969 many of these returned to the IRA to lend a hand in the defence of their community. After the violence subsided it left behind tension in the ranks of the Belfast IRA which centred on the direction the movement had taken in the last number of years. Specifically, it was felt that the IRA had failed to identify the dangers to the Catholic community inherent in the civil rights campaign and had ignored the need to arm and train for the defence of the Catholics when the inevitable confrontation took place. Considering the massive damage that had been done to Catholic homes and the huge number of families who had had to move, the IRA had obviously failed in these two main areas.

Just one week after the arrival of the British troops in Belfast in 1969 a group of republican men, unhappy with their organisation's leadership and especially with its hesitancy over arming its membership, met in a school on North King Street on the initiative of veteran republican Jimmy Steele. Those who attended were not selected or invited, but it was known who in the city felt disgruntled and who did not. The plan for the meeting spread by word of mouth.

Those present included Gerry Adams, John Kelly, Joe Cahill, and Seamus Twomey. Sinn Féin Ard Comhairle member Daithí Ó Connaill was also present. The meeting was dominated by a Belfast man who was held in high regard by the men. It was decided that the Belfast leaders Liam McMillen and Jim Sullivan should be removed as soon as possible and that work should begin on removing the Dublin leadership too, replacing it with one holding more traditional republican views. According to one who was there, Adams, one of the younger men at the meeting, was 'silent, quiet, but not passive. He did not say much, but when he did he had it all summed up. His comments were always pertinent'.

McMillen had been in prison, but when he was released he called a meeting of his supporters on 22 September in a hall above a pub on Cyprus Street, off the Falls Road. A group of sixteen men met in a hall on North King Street and, some armed with revolvers, made their way to the McMillen meeting. The group included Adams, Twomey and Kelly. They burst into the meeting as it neared its end and, after charging McMillen with failing to protect the local population, outlined their demands.

McMillen resisted and a compromise was reached: he would be allowed retain his position as leader of the Belfast Brigade, but six new members would be drafted onto his staff. Also, the Belfast IRA would cut off communication with the Dublin leadership for three months. If after these three months the leadership in Dublin had not been replaced they then would be, and a separate Northern Command would assume complete autonomy in the North. The emphasis would return to the movement's traditional military role. As a gesture of protest, Belfast would not send any members to an extraordinary IRA Army Convention which had been called for November to discuss the Sinn Féin policy of not accepting seats won in elections to either the southern or northern parliament. Lastly, the £3,500 which had been donated by the Catholic businessmen for 'relief supplies' would instead be used to purchase arms.

In early November the adjutant of B Company, Liam McParland, while on IRA business, was driving towards Belfast when his car crashed and he was fatally injured. He was said to be moving arms up to Belfast and organising a training camp when the crash occurred. The movement of arms was in contravention of Belfast Command orders and it was decided that Adams, who was alleged to have been aware of what was happening, would be 'tried' and, if found guilty, reproved. However the split in the republican movement, which saw Adams go with the Provisionals, meant that he avoided this.

McParland was the first IRA volunteer to die since the summer, but the leadership refused to sanction the traditional firing of a volley over his grave. However hours after his burial Adams and another older man, in defiance of the leadership, crept silently into the dark deserted cemetery in Milltown to give their final farewell to their fallen comrade. Adams later wrote about the event, beginning with himself and his older colleague walking down the pitch-black Whiterock Road and then 'cutting down' Milltown Row.[1]

> The moon peeked at them from behind clouds and cars on the motorway, below them, sped by unknowing and uncaring. The man with the cap [the older comrade] was breathless as they reached the hedge at Milltown Cemetery. His companion wished he hadn't worn those

bloody white trousers. The cemetery waited on them, rows and rows of serried tombstones reflecting the cold moonlight. It was desperate quiet...

They were at the Republican Plot. The older man whispered to him. Wreaths lay on the grave where they had been stretched that morning and the newly dug clay glistened where the diggers had shaped it into a ridge. The two men glanced at each other and then, silently, they stood abreast of the grave. They prayed their silent prayers and the moon, spying them from above, hid behind a cloud. The men stood to attention. A night wind crept down from the mountain and rustled its way through the wreaths. One of the men barked an order. They both raised revolvers towards the sky and three volleys of shots crashed their way over the grave and across the graveyard.

The young man was tense, a little pale. The man with the cap breathed freely. He pocketed his weapon. The younger man shoved his into the waistband of his jeans. They moved off quickly. The moon slid from behind the clouds again, the wind shook itself and swept across the landscape. All was quiet again.

For Adams it was a difficult time. He had been working with McMillen since his early teens and had been one of the most enthusiastic republican activists in the city, and the only one not to side with McMillen in the internal dispute within the republican family. He had felt very positive about much of the political activity which the movement had been promoting and was unhappy about the push to jettison this facet from republican activity. Also, he was one of the few members of the 'disgruntled' section who had been active in the years before the summer of 1969. Most of the others were older republican veterans, who had drifted away from the movement during its 1960s metamorphosis. (His parents had been among those unhappy with the way the movement had been changing.) But Adams had strong reservations about the competence of the Dublin leadership. When it became known that he was siding with the traditional, militant element, rather than with the more political, less militant side, it caused some surprise in Belfast; it was a great disappointment to McMillen and Sullivan. Nevertheless, having made his decision, Adams showed nothing but strong conviction that the grouping he had sided with was the correct one for republicans to join.

The Belfast republican community quickly broke into two separate camps, with the more militant one forming around Billy McKee as its leader. Decisions as to which camp to join were made for various reasons, not only political assessment but family and peer pressure also. In Adams' area of Ballymurphy, the forty or so republicans there put the issue to a vote. They gathered in a local hall where Sullivan and McMillen pressed their case, while Adams, who had not yet celebrated his twenty-first birthday, outlined the arguments for going with McKee. The attendance voted overwhelmingly to go with McKee.

Despite the IRA's performance during the August '69 riots, militant families like Adams' were now looked upon by the population of West Belfast as a source of leadership and protection. Coming as he did from a family of republican 'aristocrats', being well-grounded in republicanism and having been active during the summer riots, Adams found himself being looked to for leadership in his area. He quickly made obvious his organisational abilities, as he busied himself forming defence committees, meeting residents and reassuring them, travelling to Dublin to meet sympathisers with the McKee camp there and devising a new strategy.

For the fledgling group gathered around McKee the most important issue was the procurement of arms and ammunition. Veteran Belfast republican John Kelly began to make contacts in the murky world of international arms dealing in Germany, France, Holland, Czechoslovakia and the United States, opening up supply lines which in some cases are still being used by the Provisionals today. In December Kelly and another man met with Irish-Americans in the Bronx and established a funding organisation which was to develop into NORAID and provide significant funding over the following years. The Irish-Americans proved to be the most trustworthy and reliable arms suppliers in those early days.

The Rift Complete

At the 1969 Sinn Féin Ard Fheis the issue of abstentionism, which had been discussed, voted on, and rejected at previous Ard Fheiseanna, was again raised. It had been decided to commission a group to draw up a report, with recommendations on abstentionism and the possibility of Sinn Féin forming a 'National Liberation Front' with other groups on the Left, to forward left wing policies in Ireland. In October 1969 the IRA's Army Council endorsed the report's recommendation that abstentionism be abandoned. In December the IRA held an Army Convention which, as agreed at gunpoint, was not attended by any Belfast delegates. The convention voted in favour of ending abstentionism and creating a National Liberation Front. When Chief of Staff Seán MacStiofáin left at the end of the convention, he was driven straight to Belfast where he addressed a meeting of twenty IRA men who agreed to set up a new organisation in the North and to hold another Army Convention. The core group of this new IRA next met in an Irish midlands town à few days before Christmas. There they elected a 'Provisional Army Executive' of twelve, which in turn elected a 'Provisional Army Council' of seven. The term 'Provisional' was to be used until the Army Convention could be held, but by the time the meeting took place the name had become well-known, and it stuck.

At the Sinn Féin Ard Fheis in January 1970, the abstentionism motion failed to win the two-thirds majority needed to allow it to be dropped from the constitution. However, a vote of confidence in the President of Sinn Féin, Cathal Goulding, was called for. This was, in effect, a vote of support for his efforts to have abstentionism ended. As Goulding addressed the Ard Fheis, MacStiofáin grabbed a second microphone and said that Goulding no longer supported the IRA and that to support him would be against the provisions of the Sinn Féin constitution. He declared his allegiance to the Provisional Army Council and, urging delegates to follow him, walked out of the hall. He was followed by about one-third of the 257 delegates to a hall in Parnell Square which had been pre-booked and where another meeting was held.

The newly formed Provisional IRA (PIRA) took the view that a resurgence of violence in Northern Ireland was only a matter of time and that the important thing was to be ready to defend the Catholic community when that time came. The most likely catalyst for this resurgence would be the following summer's loyalist marching season, they reasoned. After the August rioting of '69, the British government had imposed a number of reforms on the Stormont parliament and this affront had annoyed the loyalist population. Some republicans even feared a coup attempt by loyalist extremists. The most urgent area was, therefore, that of defence and all the Provisionals' efforts were channelled into securing equipment and organising training. It was also decided that as soon as possible the Provisionals should expand their activities from solely providing defence to combining defence with retaliation. And lastly, when sufficiently prepared, the PIRA would launch an all-out assault on the 'occupying' British forces.[2]

Ballymurphy Riots

In August 1969 the people of Ballymurphy who had been building barricades and awaiting the next loyalist attack, had been glad of the arrival of the British army and the subsequent drop in the level of violence. However as time wore on the presence of the troops on the streets and the constant harassment and searches, combined with some outright physical and verbal abuse, led to relations between the community and the soldiers deteriorating.

A number of months after their arrival, Adams and some others were instrumental in organising a picket, mostly of local women, outside the Ballymurphy British army base, complaining about their behaviour. The soldiers reacted in a heavy-handed manner and alienated more people in the area, causing a further deterioration in relations and an increase in tension. There followed a number of outbreaks of heavy violence. During the fighting the Adams' home was one singled out for special attention and on numerous occasions Saracen armoured vehicles were driven through the front garden and up to the hall door, in an ongoing series of harassments. (Gerry Adams had not however been staying in the family home since the outbreak of violence in August '69.)

The community slowly started to reject the British army's presence and almost constant street-fighting began. In the 18 months which followed the women's protest, and almost without a shot being fired, the British army were stretched to the limit to maintain their presence in the area. At one stage an entire regiment had to be withdrawn, as the troops were suffering from fatigue. The army used thousands of canisters of CS gas,   but failed to subdue the community.

For Adams, what was happening in Ballymurphy was to remain for him one of the high points of his life. There were committees for everything – women's committees, youth committees, street committees, publicity committees. All subjects, from politics to litter to how to deal with hooligans and criminals, were thrashed out at regular meetings. He considered it an exercise in democratisation and an example of an entire community involved in a structured revolt.

The climax came in the summer of 1971 during the loyalist marching season. The people in Ballymurphy had been opposed to any march going through their area, but accepted an assurance from the authorities that there would be no singing of loyalist songs or playing of loyalist tunes as the marches went through nationalist areas. However, during the first march through Ballymurphy a loyalist played Orange songs while the British troops provided protection. In the eyes of the nationalists the soldiers had broken their promise and shown their true sympathies. It marked the complete breakdown of relations between the two communities.

Fierce rioting broke out and in the following weeks over fifteen people were killed in Ballymurphy. (Some died later from wounds received during the fighting.) The IRA organised the street-fighters as best they could. At each riot there were people with wet sacks to put on top of smoking gas canisters and others armed with hurley sticks to 'puck' back an incoming canister or to use as a weapon in hand-to-hand fighting. Basins of water and vinegar were placed outside innumerable houses in Ballymurphy, to wet handkerchiefs or faces during the CS gas attacks. Front and back doors were left open so rioters could make their escape during army swoops. An attempt to establish an RUC station in the heart of the area was prevented by local people who overran the intended site. On another occasion the rioters overcame the British troops and drove off in some of their jeeps. One day during some fierce rioting the soldiers fired a number of canisters of gas into the Adams' home. Dominic Adams, who was five years old at the time, was taken from the house unconscious. Such was the amount of gas in the small house that no one could live in it for many days afterwards and clothes that were in the house during the attack stank of the gas for weeks.

Despite the misgivings of the British top brass, internment, which had been sought for some time by the unionist politicians, was finally approved on 3 August 1971. At 4am on the morning of Tuesday, 10 August, 'Operation Demetrius' was launched. Fifteen people died in the ensuing violence. 342 men were arrested, but about one-third of these were released within two days. Adams, like most of those in the 'Provisional' republican movement in the North, had been informed the day before that internment was about to be introduced and had spent the night warning people in the Ballymurphy area. When the British paratroopers swooped down on his family home, he watched the operation from a nearby estate. He saw the soldiers drag out his barefooted father in his pyjamas, and his younger brother Liam, who was in his early teens and too young to be detained. Liam was later released, but Paddy Adams was badly beaten and then interned. While the father and son were taken away, the paratroopers remained and all but demolished the Adams' home: they smashed ornaments and defecated on beds, in wardrobes, on the floor and wherever else they felt like. Anne Adams, Gerry's mother, had to find a new house for her family while her husband was interned in Long Kesh. They never returned to their former home. It was later demolished.

Onto the Offensive

By the end of January 1970, the two now-rival IRA groupings in Belfast – the Provisionals and the Officials, as they had been dubbed respectively – had organised themselves. Recruitment was slow to both organisations at first, but as disenchantment with the British troops grew, so too did the numbers attracted to the paramilitary groups.

Following an outbreak of serious violence involving firearms in Belfast in late June, the British began a series of house raids in the Lower Falls, an area dominated by the Officials, in the hope of uncovering arms dumps. The Officials decided they could not stand by and watch their arms being taken. They began to fight back. The fighting was fierce and by Friday, 3 July, there were 3,000 troops in the area, supported by numerous armoured cars and helicopters. Later that night, as full-scale riots raged, a curfew was declared and the troops began a house-to-house search which resulted in the recovery of a large quantity of firearms, explosives, ammunition and equipment. During the search, the soldiers acted with a new ferocity.

Ironically, while almost all the confiscated arms and explosives belonged to the Officials, the hatred of the British army led to an increase in recruits to the Provisionals. To the recruits, the Provisionals offered a better chance of getting involved in the fighting.

Whereas the typical recruit to the IRA prior to 1969 would most likely have come from a family with a tradition of republicanism and have been thoroughly grounded in the history and ethos of the IRA before being accepted into the ranks, a growing number of PIRA volunteers in 1970 and 1971 came from 'ordinary' working-class families. Most recruits were young men and women who had witnessed the events of the previous year or two, and who felt the urge to join up and fight back. The Falls curfew led to a significant increase in the numbers wanting to join, as did the shooting dead of two innocent, unarmed youths, Seamus Cusack and Desmond Beattie, in Derry in July 1971 and, or course, the introduction of internment one month later. With the rapid deterioration of the relationship between the troops and the nationalist population, the PIRA decided that it could mount an increasingly violent campaign without damaging its support base among the nationalist working-class.

Day to day life in Northern Ireland, and especially in Belfast, had undergone a dramatic transformation during 1970, when the IRA had pursued its campaign of bombing 'economic targets'. This policy had been decided on at the earliest Provisional strategy meetings and as well as increasing the cost to the British exchequer of their presence in Northern Ireland, it was designed to draw security resources away from the Catholic ghettos and into the city centres. Visiting Belfast city centre now involved submitting to a series of body and vehicle checks. The bombing campaign was to lead to the slaughter of many civilians over the coming years, and the terrible maiming of many more.

It was not until early 1971 that the Provisionals felt strong enough to go on the offensive against the British and that the nationalist population was ready to stomach cold-blooded killing of the hated troops. On Friday, 5 February, the first British soldier to die from a PIRA bullet was shot in Belfast. He was Gunner Robert Curtis, a 20-year-old soldier with the 94th Locating Regiment of the Royal Artillery. He was shot in the New Lodge district by a republican who was himself to die before the end of the year.

On the same day as Gunner Curtis died, British troops shot dead their first PIRA man during rioting between Catholics and Protestants in the Old Park area of West Belfast. He was James Saunders, a 22-year-old bakery worker.

The killing power of the PIRA increased quickly and in the reckless zeal to inflict casualties, 'codes of war', which had earlier been expected of IRA volunteers, began to fall by the wayside. On a night in early March, three British soldiers were to die in circumstances which caused particular revulsion.

Three young soldiers – brothers John and Douglas Craig, both in their late teens, and Douglas McCaughey – met up with three men from Belfast while drinking in a city centre bar. They all moved to another bar and at the end of the night piled into cars to go to a party where, the Belfast men said, there would be plenty of women. On a quiet stretch of road up over the city, the cars stopped and the men got out to relieve themselves. As the soldiers urinated, with their beer bottles clutched in their hands, they were shot in the head by their IRA drinking companions. When the bodies were found, one brother was lying on top of the other. McCaughey was propped up by the embankment, still holding his beer. The killings were in contravention of an IRA standing order that soldiers be on duty when attacked, but that rule was in time completely dismissed by the Provisionals. Indeed, the promise of female companionship was to be used again to lure unsuspecting British servicemen to their deaths.

Guerrilla Warfare

From August 1969 to early 1971, Gerry Adams lived a 'scarlet pimpernel' existence as the PIRA conducted a guerrilla war against the hated British army. The existence of internment meant he had to scurry around his native city, using false names and sometimes hiding in friendly houses for days on end. He was one of the most wanted men on the British army's list of republicans. While 'Operation Demetrius' initially failed to round up many Provisionals of consequence, with most of those detained being older republicans no longer active, or political activists involved in civil rights or welfare activities, as the months progressed more and more of the PIRA's leaders were captured. As the leaders were detained, their deputies took command.

Adams quickly established himself as a valuable organiser and planner, with a reputation for being energetic and intelligent. The scale of the killing in Belfast was at its height, and horror followed horror. The republican movement came under great pressure as the might of the British army and the local security forces were turned against it. As older, more senior Belfast republicans found themselves being picked up and interned, an increasing burden of responsibility fell upon Adams.

In the midst of all this he began to court Colette McArdle of Belfast, whom he had met during the summer of 1969. It was not until July 1971 that they started to 'go out' together, but after just six weeks of courtship they got married (during 'Internment Week', the week of heavy fighting that followed the introduction of internment). The service was in a Belfast church. For their honeymoon the couple went to Dublin for forty-eight hours and then, for Adams, it was back to life on the run.

Internment released a massive wave of indignation and bitterness among nationalists, followed by a huge burst of violence. The Provisionals launched an all-out bombing campaign and dropped the last vestiges of restraint they had put on their deadly activity. All members of the RUC and Ulster Defence Regiment (the UDR which had replaced the hated B Specials after the 1969 riots) now became 'legitimate' targets, whether on or off duty. In the five months after internment, ninety-seven people died in the violence.

In Derry the army and RUC were run out of the Catholic areas of the Bogside and Creggan, and 'Free Derry' was established. On Sunday, 30 January 1972, British soldiers attacked and opened fire on unarmed civil rights marchers in the city and killed thirteen of them. Seven of those killed were under 19 years of age. Adams was in the Republic when he heard news of the slaughter on the radio and immediately began to drive to Belfast, the death toll mounting on radio reports as he made his way northwards. In the Republic the government declared a national day of mourning. Three days after what became known as 'Bloody Sunday' an angry crowd in Dublin burnt down the British Embassy.

The British Prime Minister, Edward Heath, decided to strip Stormont of its powers of law and order. Britain was receiving a slating in the international news media. There were allegations of torture by the British army on detained republican prisoners at Palace Barracks. The Irish government was later to take the British to the Court of Human Rights in The Hague, which found that scientific 'sensory deprivation' experiments had been carried out on fourteen internees, among them Liam Hannaway, a cousin of Adams.

By early 1972, less than three years since its inception, the Provisional IRA had developed the capacity to mount a widespread campaign of violence, and had helped raise nationalist and republican feeling throughout the island to a fervour.

5: 'Most Wanted' Man

When the Lenadoon confrontation exploded, causing MacStiofáin to admit that the 1972 truce was effectively over, Gerry Adams immediately went back on the run. Following his brief respite at his parents' home with his wife, he now found himself back living in various 'safe houses' or 'billets' (the homes of families with republican sympathies who are unlikely to be raided by the army or police), where he stayed for periods of varying length, from a few weeks to several months.

Sometimes he had to remain in his room almost all the time. Unless there was good reason to be out late, he would usually try be back in his billet before dark, when it became more dangerous for such a wanted man to be out on the streets of Belfast. One street where he stayed for about three or four months was raided on a number of occasions by the British army, with Adams always making his getaway over back walls and down alleyways.

There were many narrow escapes with the security forces during this, his second period of life on the run. The British put a high priority on his capture. One day a large photograph of his face was published on the front page of a British tabloid newspaper, which described him as the man 'most wanted' by the British. Adams discovered this when he went into a shop in West Belfast to buy a packet of cigarettes, only to notice his picture lying on the counter. He quickly hid his face as best he could without looking too suspicious, and made his way down the Falls Road to a safe house.

One night he failed to get back to his billet before dark and was hurrying along when, as he came around a bend in the road, he ran straight into a British paratrooper. Normally when making his way up long winding roads he would cross continually so as to be able to see around the bend ahead; if there were soldiers, he would go off down a side street. But this night, in his haste, he had not done so. The soldier shouted at him to stop, and raised and pointed his rifle. Adams reacted in a jocose way, telling the soldier to 'catch yourself on' and slagging him for being so nervous. He answered the soldier's questions and having satisfied him, went slowly on up the road, his heart pounding. He knew that if there was one paratrooper on the street there most likely were scores of them. Once out of sight of the trooper, he broke into a sprint and ran home as fast as he could, without being stopped again.

Another day he was travelling from Beechmount to Divis Street on a double-decker bus, sitting in the front upstairs seat reading a book by the Irish poet Seamus Heaney. The bus was stopped by soldiers for a check. Adams had long hair and a beard, and was wearing a fashionable 'maxi' coat which came down almost to his ankles. The soldiers boarded the bus and looked at all the passengers, asking some of them questions. When they got to Adams, they stopped and asked him his name. He gave the false name he was using and managed to satisfy the soldiers that he was who he said he was. They left and the bus again began to make its way towards Divis Street. When it neared the stop where Adams was to get off, he stood up and walked down the aisle to the stairs. To his astonishment, he found that the passengers were smiling knowingly at him, giving him the thumbs-up sign and feigning wiping the sweat off their foreheads. One of the highest names on the British Army's wanted list, he had not quite melted into the crowd to the extent he imagined he had!

Bloody Friday

Just under two weeks after the ending of the 1972 truce the IRA showed just what it meant when its leader Seán MacStiofáin had promised to resume the campaign 'with the utmost ferocity and ruthlessness'.[1] On 21 July the IRA hid twenty-two bombs in the centre of Belfast in an operation planned by the Belfast leadership, that was immediately to be dubbed 'Bloody Friday'. Beginning shortly after lunch, and lasting for about an hour and a quarter, the bombs went off one by one, killing nine people, injuring many more and causing mass panic in the centre of Belfast. The greatest number of casualites from a single bomb happened in the Oxford Street bus station, where a crowd, fleeing from nearby Albert Bridge where they had heard there was a bomb, ran straight into the bomb hidden in the bus station. It exploded, killing six people, including two teenage boys. Many of those killed or injured were dismembered by the blasts. The IRA accepted responsibility for the carnage, but claimed that their warnings had been ignored. In fact, the IRA had given a plethora of warnings, causing widespread confusion. There was outrage throughout the island of Ireland and widespread disgust with the IRA. For the Northern Ireland Secretary of State, William Whitelaw, the killings tipped the balance. He gave in to the army pressure which he had been resisting and gave permission for the invasion of Free Derry. Ten days after Bloody

Friday, 'Operation Motorman' was launched.

Adams was in a billet on the Falls Road, lying on a mattress reading Frank O'Connor's 'Oedipus Complex' and enjoying it heartily on the morning of 'Operation Motorman'. He was sure that the British would launch some sort of response to the killings in Belfast on Bloody Friday and was not surprised when the woman who lived in the house returned from early mass, saying there were British troops everywhere. Later Adams and the men he was sharing the house with went out to survey the scene in the city. The British were indeed out in force. The high numbers of troops on Belfast's streets over the coming months meant he had to all but confine himself to the house where he was staying, venturing out only very occasionally for specific tasks and almost always having to return before 6 pm.

The intensity of the period and its effect on him he only noticed at the end of the occasional brief breaks he would take in the Republic where he would meet up with his wife. It was then, when he returned from this relative relaxation to the fighting and being on the run in Belfast, that he noticed the strain of the life he was leading.

The level of casualties in 1972 was to be the highest in the whole decade and often comrades he had spoken to only minutes before would go out to die on the streets of Belfast in a hail of bullets. Against the strain and tragedy however was balanced the conviction and intense camaraderie which existed among the men and women fighting a war and living a 'pimpernel' existence for a cause they believed in, in the heart of the working-class community where they grew up.

Increasing Prominence

The British government were hoping that the abolition of Stormont, the introduction of direct rule from Westminster and a number of reforms would go some way towards satisfying the Catholic community, thereby taking from the IRA the bulk of their support and sympathy.

In addition a new party to represent the nationalist community was formed – the Social and Democratic Labour Party (SDLP). It called on the community to reject the IRA and its campaign of violence and support their party's efforts to find a peaceful solution to the problems of the six counties. The IRA considered the SDLP a party of 'Uncle Toms', but they represented a section of the Catholic population which roundly condemned as wrong the actions of the IRA. And this section was growing with every IRA atrocity.

In the Republic, the swing in attitudes was such that by the spring of 1972 the government introduced Part V of the Offences against the State Act, under which a suspected IRA member could be convicted on the evidence of a senior Garda (police) officer saying the suspect was a member of the IRA, unless that is, the suspect denied that this was so. IRA volunteers at the time were refusing to recognise the courts and so no rebuttals were given, resulting in automatic convictions. Special three-judge non-jury courts were set up for hearing IRA trials.

In November 1972 Chief of Staff MacStiofáin was picked up in Dublin and charged with being a member of the IRA. He immediately went on a hunger- and thirst-strike. He was tried and found guilty and sent to Mountjoy Prison in Dublin, where he continued his protest. His condition deteriorated rapidly and he was transferred to the Army Hospital in the Curragh, Co. Kildare. As he approached death, there was a surge of republican sympathy throughout the Republic, accompanied by large demonstrations in Dublin. The army was put on stand-by in case the situation became too violent for the Gardaí alone. However, when a priest who had been regularly visiting MacStiofáin urged him to end his fast, to avoid bloodshed on the streets of Ireland that night, the IRA leader ended his protest. But not to persist in such a protest was to undermine its effectiveness in general and MacStiofáin's standing in the republican movement was seriously undermined.

MacStiofáin had upset his colleagues in another way too. It is IRA policy that no matter what rank a man or woman holds within the organisation, once inside jail they revert to being an ordinary volunteer and take orders from the elected officers commanding in the prison. But when in Mountjoy, MacStiofáin refused to take orders from the OC there. After his release, he was never to hold the position of Chief of Staff again.

In late 1972 Adams, who was now a figure of importance within the republican movement both in the six counties and in the Republic, was the senior member of the movement in his native Belfast. In January while MacStiofáin was on his protest in the Army Hospital in the Curragh, Adams was one of a three-man team responsible for running political affairs. He had special responsibility for affairs in the six counties.

Bombing Britain

Soon after 'Operation Motorman', General Sir Frank King was appointed Officer Commanding the British troops in Northern Ireland. Under his leadership the army changed its tactics, using large numbers of undercover units to swamp republican areas such as West Belfast in massive intelligence-gathering operations. These operations led to increasing success in 'lifting' paramilitaries. Army intelligence also began to feed out false stories to the media in order to create tension, friction and loss of morale within republican ranks.

In addition, a number of legislative changes were introduced to assist the authorities in their fight. Following the publication of a report compiled by a British law lord, Lord Diplock, changes were introduced on the acceptance of evidence and the procedures for arrest, as well as one-judge non-jury courts which came to be known as 'Diplock Courts'. The courts were ostensibly introduced to deal with the problem of the IRA and other paramilitary groups intimidating, or even killing, jury members and witnesses, though republicans claimed the courts were introduced simply to allow their members be convicted more easily.

The new British tactics increased their success in fighting the republicans, who found their leaders were being picked up with increasing frequency. With the heavy surveillance and high risk of known republicans being caught or shot, young volunteers were carrying out more and more of the fighting. Senior figures such as Adams had to constantly shift from place to place, while at all times keeping an eye out for the British troops.

IRA atrocities, and particularly the killings on Bloody Friday, were creating revulsion among the nationalist population. This swing against the IRA was aided by British intelligence which fed out 'black propaganda' to discredit the movement. British intelligence agents also arranged for the carrying out of IRA 'mistakes' to further discredit the movement.

Moreover, the lack of success of the 'economic bombings' campaign, coupled with the increasing success of the British army in picking up volunteers, led to a rethink on strategy within the northern leadership. The IRA began to opt increasingly for well-planned sniping operations instead of extended open shoot-outs with the British. To the extent that the numbers of soldiers killed by the IRA dropped steadily in the coming years from the high point of 1972 (103 soldiers killed), the new strategy was not a success.

But new avenues were being explored. At an Army Council meeting in June 1972 at Blackrock, Co. Dublin, the idea of extending the bombing campaign to Britain was discussed, though it was not until early 1973 that formal approval was given to such a plan. The death and havoc in Northern Ireland was not sufficient to drive the British out, it was concluded, so something greater and nearer home was needed to convince the British. The campaign, despite its total failure to achieve its objectives, was to continue over the coming years and cause a high level of casualties and disgust. Most of those killed were civilians.

In the summer of 1974 a group which was to become known as the Balcombe Street bombers, moved to Britain and began a ghastly campaign of bombings and death. The worst single incident – not the work of the 'Balcombe Street' unit – came on the night of Thursday, 21 November 1974, when two bombs were placed in two city centre bars in Birmingham packed with young people. The explosions killed twenty-one and injured 162. Six men were subsequently charged and convicted for this outrage, but very strong doubts persist about the justness of their convictions.

Abstention

The British government published a White Paper in March 1973 containing details of a Northern Ireland Assembly, which they were proposing as a solution to the seemingly insurmountable political problem. A seventy-eight-member parliament would be elected by proportional representation and the elected members would vote for a Prime Minister, who, in turn, would select a cabinet, to include a proportion of members of the leading opposition party. The Executive would have limited powers at first and London would retain control of security. A Council of Ireland, which would operate as a link between the government of the Republic and the Northern Assembly, was also proposed.

The SDLP gave the White Paper proposal a cautious welcome. But the IRA, intent as it was on breaking the connection with Britain and creating a united Ireland, saw the proposal as a device allowing the British to maintain their foothold in Ireland. The President of Sinn Féin, Ruairí Ó Brádaigh, wanted republicans to contest the elections being held in Northern Ireland that year, in order to give a voice to those who objected to the Union and supported the IRA. But many of the northern members of the Army Council were against the idea, believing that all their resources should be devoted to fighting. Also, the risk of their not receiving a significant vote, of being humiliated at the polls, was too great, they said. As a result the district council elections in Northern Ireland and the new Assembly elections in 1973 both went ahead without Sinn Féin contesting them.

6: Brownie's Long War

In July 1973 Adams was in a house on the Falls Road with some colleagues when they became suspicious of some men sitting in a car parked on the other side of the road. A man was sent to contact the local IRA unit and ask them to go and check out the suspicious car. Adams and the other men in the house looked on as the IRA unit approached the car, had a few words with its occupants and then walked away again. The people in the car then drove off.

What the men in the house did not know was that when the IRA unit had knocked on the window of the car, the occupants had produced sub-machine-guns and told them to clear off. The unit, who had been told at second hand to go check the car, did not know where Adams and his colleagues were hiding out, and so could not immediately warn them that the car contained undercover British soldiers.

Later, news came to the house that there were British troops everywhere and that they seemed to have the area sealed off. Adams and another man checked out the backyard and discovered that there were British troops concealed at the opposite end. They decided the British were hoping that the obviously suspicious car would cause them to sneak out the back, into a hail of bullets. Whatever the truth of that, they waited in the house and soon a British foot patrol came to the door – without visiting any of the other houses on the street – and arrested Adams, Brendan Hughes and Tom Cahill, a brother of the well-known republican Joe Cahill. It was learned later that another man who had been with them in the house and had left, had been followed and arrested some distance away.

The soldiers had simply walked in, touched each of the three men lightly on the shoulder and said 'I am arresting you', to each of them in turn. Adams casually lit his pipe using a rolled up piece of paper. It was a mistake on the soldiers' part to allow him do so: the paper contained the only incriminating evidence in the building.

The men were taken to Springfield Road RUC Station and badly beaten by members of the British army. Adams was brought into a room where a number of British soldiers in plain clothes put him spread-eagled against the wall and began to deliver blows to his

kidneys and genitals. He swung around at his attackers and broke
a wrist-watch belonging to one of them. This seemed to fuel their
anger and they beat him until he fell unconscious. A bucket of water
was thrown over him to revive him and the beating continued.
During the assault, which lasted several hours, he was stripped
naked and one of the army officers, in what Adams thought was an
echo of the exchange he had had with Whitelaw a year earlier in
London, said, 'Yes Gerry, all bets are off'.

During a pause in the beating he was put sitting hunkered in the
corner of the room, and the bucket used for throwing water over
him put over his head. Cigarettes were extinguished on the backs
of his hands. After he was left alone, one of the two uniformed
soldiers left to guard him said to the other, 'I don't think that sort
of thing is right'. The colleague replied, 'Ah, fuck him'.

A British army doctor came and gave Adams a medical examination and, having pronounced him strong enough, the beatings
continued. The soldiers were looking for information, but to their
repeated questions Adams simply replied, 'I'm sorry, I can't help
you'. The response seemed to infuriate the troops and Adams was
knocked unconscious on a number of occasions as the punches and
kicks rained down on him. Afterwards, he was covered in bruises
and his kidneys had suffered damage from which they never
completely recovered.

The beatings ended as quickly as they had begun; suddenly the
soldiers, who had spent the last number of hours trying to beat
information out of him, were drying his clothes on the boiler and
brushing his hair. He and the two other republican prisoners were
brought outside and lined up with their British captors for a football
team-type photograph. Hughes had to be carried such was the
severity of the beating he had endured; the soldiers had made him
sit on a spiked chain. This taking of photographs was a common
event with prisoners of note, and it was believed that the troops had
organised a sort of informal lottery, with prizes going to the captors
of selected figures. There was money riding on both Adams and
Hughes.

The three men were then taken in a convoy to Castlereagh
Detention Centre, each captive being transported in a separate
armoured car. Adams was put with one hand 'cuffed to the inside
roof of the vehicle and the other handcuffed to a plain-clothes
soldier who held a cocked Browning pistol to his head throughout
the trip and had threatened, 'If we are ambushed, you are going
first'.

When the three men had first been picked up on the Falls Road, a number of people had gathered aggressively around the British arresting party, and a group of women, including Adams' wife, Colette, had gathered outside Springfield Road Barracks when the men were brought there. However, the women dispersed after the early evening news said that the arrested men had been transferred to Castlereagh. In fact the trio were still inside the barracks and were not transferred until much later. Adams had allegedly been one of fourteen top republicans lifted by the British in Belfast that day, according to media reports quoting security sources.

Army success in arresting leading Provos lead to something of a crisis with the movement.[1] Following a meeting of IRA leaders in the Republic, a statement was issued saying that all the positions would be quickly filled and the IRA campaign would continue unabated. Within forty-eight hours there were media reports in Belfast that the empty leadership positions had been filled.

The plain-clothes men who had been involved in the arrest of Adams and his comrades had been noted by the IRA men on the Falls Road. One of them, who had also been involved in beating Adams, was shortly afterwards shot dead by the IRA in an unrelated incident.

Adams was brought to an interrogation room at Castlereagh, but little effort was made to question him. His RUC and British army captors spent most of their time playing cards and filling in crossword puzzles. The three men were later transferred to Long Kesh and put into Cage 6. Just one year after he had been released for negotiations with the British government, Adams was back again 'behind the wire'.

Escape Officer

This time he was determined to escape. He immediately began to look for possible routes out of the camp and on his first day there he spotted one. The food lorry, which each day entered the cages and then was driven out of the camp, could provide a possible escape route, he decided. If a man could be concealed under its chassis, there was a strong likelihood that he would be carried unnoticed straight out the Long Kesh gates.

Preparations began immediately. Another prisoner in Cage 6, Paul Marlowe (an ex-British paratrooper who has since been killed), oversaw the making of a harness which, it was planned, would be hooked to the lorry's underbelly. While perfecting it, Hughes, who had been chosen for the escape and who was still bruised from the beating he had suffered on the day he was picked up, was hung upside-down in the harness under his bunk, while Marlowe made final adjustments. A 'blind spot' had been noted where, it was thought, a man might be able to slip under the lorry without being detected. However, it was later decided that it was too dangerous. The people in the next cage believed they could get a man under the lorry without his being noticed and so the harness was passed on to them. An inmate in that cage, Mark Graham, did manage to get into the harness under the lorry undetected, but his back was broken as the truck travelled over the security ramps in the camp. He was later released and is now confined to a wheel-chair.

Adams' determination to escape was not diminished by the tragic outcome of that first attempt. He went to the camp OC and informed him that he would continue trying. He felt that the only way to continue fighting the British while in a camp like Long Kesh was to escape. Non-co-operation with the British and fighting with them inside the camp was doomed to failure; it only resulted in the inmates being beaten up. Adams was made escape officer of an escape committee which was formed and a systematic examination of the camp began, with all possibilities being noted and classified. The camp population was transformed into one big team, intent on the possibility of escape. The escape ethos became firmly established and a steady series of attempts, some of them successful, began.

Camp Activity

Life in the camp was hard, especially in Cage 6. There were constant raids by the British soldiers, and these often developed into fist fights, which the troops almost always won. At times the inmates would be brought out to the wire and put standing against it, spread-eagled, with their legs back from the wire and their hands resting on it. They might be left there for hours on end, a painful experience, particularly on cold dark nights with the prisoners dressed only in their underwear. It was this sort of experience which convinced Adams that the only fight you could win against the British while in Long Kesh was the battle to escape. It was only when the British went too far in their harassment that it made sense to respond, to resist. To plot for escape, and to work on political education, seemed to him the best ways of forwarding the struggle while incarcerated. During his time there, the system of education for prisoners began to be formalised. Inmates in the camp also occupied themselves with craftwork, making leather wallets and St Brigid's crosses, but Adams never got involved in this.

Escape Again

A second escape was planned and Hughes was again selected as the man to go. The escape itself was simple but ingenious, though the back-up required was considerable, since Hughes needed time to get well away before his absence was noticed. Cage 6 was reserved for the high-security inmates and being in the centre of the camp was the subject of special observation.

Hughes was wrapped in thick cloth and put in an old mattress, which was then sown up again and thrown out on the rubbish heap at the cage gate just before the time for the collection. The mattress was thrown onto the back of the lorry along with the rest of the rubbish and taken along to the dump outside the camp. Left at the dump, Hughes waited for some time, then cut himself out of the mattress and reported back for active service.

Hughes had had to be dumped at a rubbish heap outside the gate of a cage other than Cage 6, so it was necessary to sneak him to this cage before he took his place in the mattress. Also, another prisoner had to slip into Cage 6 to take Hughes' place, so that the correct number of inmates would be in the cage during the frequent counts it was subjected to. Sometime after the escape, the prisoners were able to sneak the man who had taken Hughes' place back to his own cage, without being caught. Later, to the great amusement of the Long Kesh inmates, Hughes placed a notice in the *Irish News*, the nationalist newspaper in Belfast, which contained a greeting to the chief prison officer in the camp, Davey Long, followed by an insult.

The prisoners were greatly heartened by their success in slipping Hughes out so soon after his arrival in the camp. But what they did not know until later was that all rubbish leaving Long Kesh is systematically spiked by the British and that Hughes had been fortunate in not being lanced as he lay inside the mattress.

Adams was chosen as the man to escape next. However, when Ivor Bell was picked up and brought to Long Kesh, it was decided that he would take Adams' place. It was felt that a man who had just been picked up was of greater value outside than a man who had been in Long Kesh for a time, since he would be more aware of the current situation on the ground. So, the night Bell arrived he was told by his friend Adams that he would be out again in a few weeks.

The escape plan was again simple and audacious. Adams was to have taken the place of an internee who had applied for parole in order to get married. He had for some time been practising trying to walk and act like the man and had found that wearing the man's boots helped greatly in mimicking his walk. This plan was now abandoned in favour of one to get Bell out. A different man applied for parole on the same basis and Bell began preparing to take his place.

The plan involved precise timing and quite a number of prisoners, only a few of whom were told exactly what was happening. The parolee whose place Bell was going to take was in Cage 5, which was quite a distance from Cage 6 and involved getting through some intervening fences and gates. It had to be organised that Bell be taken to this cage, while another man slipped into Cage 6 to take his place and the man who had applied for parole being tied up and hidden somewhere.

When the day came, the plan worked smoothly and Bell was able to walk unhindered straight out of the camp. The prisoners managed to cover for him for about two days and when at last the replacement returned to his own cage and the prison officers discovered they were a man short in Cage 6, it caused great consternation. Head prison officer Long realised he had not seen Bell for some time and ran straight to his hut. He met a prisoner at the door of the hut, who asked him what he wanted. 'Ivor, are you there,' shouted the prisoner into the hut, and said that the head prison officer wanted to see him. 'Tell him I'll be out in ten minutes,' came the reply. Outside, the prison officer's face took on an expression of relief: inside the hut, the prisoners were trying not to laugh out loud.

There was absolute euphoria in the camp after Bell's successful escape such a short time after his capture. Two important captives had escaped from under the noses of the British. However, the euphoria was dampened down considerably when Bell was picked up again a short time later and returned to Long Kesh.

Adams was personally involved in numerous escape attempts, none of them successful. Most were abandoned when it became evident that they were not going to work. On two occasions he was caught trying to escape and was later tried and sentenced to four and a half years in prison for these attempts.

The first of these took place on Christmas Eve 1973 and involved Adams and three other men, Marshall Francis Mooney, Thomas John Tolan and Martin Thomas O'Rawe, all from Belfast, trying to cut their way through fences and crawl along a tunnel of razor wire which lay in the division between the camp for sentenced prisoners and that for internees and detainees. Once in the tunnel they could travel along and escape without encountering any walls. To get out of Cage 6 was a major operation, since it was observed by two watchtowers with searchlights, one of them equipped with a general-purpose machine-gun. But the foursome managed to escape the cage without detection. They had put on heavy, dark clothing, as protection against the razor wire. Unfortunately for the would-be escapers, a slight fog descended, not enough to give them cover but sufficient to excite the security forces and cause them to put on extra guards.

When the extra security was mounted the four prisoners were lying in the wire tunnel between the two camps. There was a catwalk within feet of where they were and they were between two watchtowers. A prison warder started to patrol back and forth on the catwalk. Another two began to patrol the cage right next to where the four were lying. It had been decided earlier that when the time for midnight mass came, they would lie still, but now with the extra security patrolling so close to them it was decided to lie still until the mass, soon to begin, was over. By then, perhaps the fog would have lifted and the level of security relaxed again.

The two warders on the other side of the wire were patrolling around the huts inside the cage and the would-be escapers were listening to their steps to gauge when they would be in and out of their line of sight. The plan was that once the mass was over they would inch forward even if the warders were still there, moving whenever they were out of sight of the guards.

However, they were not to get a chance to put the plan into action. One of the warders noticed the man up ahead of Adams, Marshall Mooney, and was heard to say to his colleague, 'What's that over there?' 'It's only an old football,' his colleague replied and the two continued on their rounds. There was, in fact, a football some way ahead of Mooney, which had been kicked over the wire and not recovered. However, when the warders came around again, the more sharp-eyed one stopped, and said he was sure he could see something in the razor wire besides the ball. Knowing the game was up, Mooney made his way out of the roll of wire, stood up and started to shout 'Ho! ho! ho! Merry Christmas to you all!'

Almost immediately, the whole camp erupted into chaos – running and shouting men, barking dogs, searchlights and sirens. Mooney walked along the wire, hoping desperately that he might be able to draw attention away from where his three comrades were still hiding. The warders were telling Mooney to 'get back in here', from the other side of the wire, but when Mooney started to cut a hole in the wire with his cutters, the warders shouted at him to stop. Mooney kept walking away from his colleagues, but the ploy was doomed to failure.

In a last desperate attempt, Adams also stood up and began to walk away from where his two colleagues were trying to hide. Even greater consternation broke out. Army dogs on the other side of the wire were barking furiously. The men in the tunnel were noticed and all four were told that if they did not come back out the way they had gone in, the dogs would be released to attack them. The prisoners complied with the British demand and made their way back into the camp.

Mooney and, to a lesser extent, Adams were beaten as they were pushed and shoved up towards the punishment cells by the angry soldiers and warders. The heavy clothing they were wearing against injury from the razor wire provided them with some protection from the blows and the snapping dogs, but Adams had his glasses tied to his head and when a soldier pulled at them they ripped deeply into the skin at the side of his nose. The other two men, Tolan and O'Rawe, escaped being hit because Tolan, using a British accent, screamed and shouted at O'Rawe and marched him angrily up to the punishment cells. It confused the warders and soldiers sufficiently to allow them reach the cells in safety.

The four men were stripped naked and put in separate cells in the punishment block. The cells opened onto a long corridor where the soldiers had left their dogs loose. The prisoners shouted quips to each other and laughed and joked excitedly, but they feared that the British would now give them a serious beating, perhaps even kill them. However nothing happened during the night apart from two army officers coming to have a look at them. On Christmas Day they were visited by an army doctor who gave them a medical examination, but paid little attention to Adams' ripped face. A few days later they were allowed return to their cage.

The failed attempt had a less discouraging epilogue. Just as they were discovered, they had managed to hide an excellent wire cutters they had built at the bottom of a fence and this was later successfully recovered. Also, when they had been brought up to the punishment cells, one of them had managed to hide some equipment there before being stripped and collect it again just as he was being brought back down to his cage. The salvaged equipment was produced after they arrived back in the hut, much to the delight of their comrades.

The second attempt in which Adams was caught was another daring 'swap' escape, in July of 1974. It was noticed that a visitor who came to see Ivor Bell had something of a resemblance to Adams. The idea was hatched that if Adams could be switched for the man during a visit, he might be able to walk out to freedom. Adams' hair and beard were cut to make him look like the visitor and he doffed a wig and false beard. The visitor was seized and taken to a house where his hair was dyed to resemble Adams'. The exceedingly demanding operation involved Adams going up to meet someone who had come to visit him, slipping into Bell's visiting box when the warders were not looking, taking off his wig and beard, putting on clothes similar to those of the visitor and then walking out of the camp. The switch, strip and change, amazingly enough, were accomplished. But it was not until Adams was beside Bell's visitor that it was noticed he was a good deal shorter than Adams, who is over six feet tall. As Adams went to walk out of the prison, the difference in height was noticed and he was apprehended.

Later Adams, O'Rawe and Bell, who were also involved in the 'swap' escape attempt, as well as two young women who were involved in planning the escape bid, all received jail sentences for their trouble. Adams, who had been given eighteen months for his Christmas '73 escape bid, got another three years. Charges of alleged intimidation of another man who was involved in the escape plan were dropped when the case came to court.

Sentenced Prisoner

In 1975 when Adams was transferred to the sentenced prisoners' camp to to serve his sentences of a minimum of two years, he decided that he would divorce himself from much of the cage and camp activity and direct his energies to reading, writing and learning Irish. He wanted to snatch a period of relative peace and quiet and consider how 'the struggle' was progressing. He was sent to Cage 11, where he discovered there was a minor schism causing some unrest among the inmates there. He was asked to be OC of the cage, since it was felt that he could bring all the men together. After some resistance he agreed, but only on condition that his acceptance would not involve his being dragged into every minor issue that arose in the cage.

When he arrived in the sentenced prisoners' camp he was struck by the solemn, almost monastic atmosphere which, it seemed to him, existed there and contrasted greatly with the more happy-go-lucky spirit among the internees and detainees. The IRA administration in the sentenced end ran their camp along very militaristic and regimented lines, more like those of a regular army than what Adams considered a revolutionary force. There was little political content to the life there and instead of discipline arising out of political commitment, it was drilled into the prisoners by the militaristic regime.

Although he did not intend getting involved in the running of the cage or camp, life in Cage 11 began to change soon after Adams became its OC. A more political, more educational and more relaxed atmosphere replaced the old militaristic one. However the central role of physical force remained as before; in 1976 a home-made mortar was discovered in Cage 11 and this led to the re-introduction of strip-searching of prisoners during searches of the camp compounds. Among the inmates of Cage 11 were Bobby Sands, Brendan MacFarlane, Larry Marley, Brendan Hughes and Danny Lennon, men who were later to become widely known for various reasons. A process of political education based on discussions developed, as did an informal review of republican strategy and belief. Among the projects discussed and developed was the creation of a system of 'peoples' assemblies' and the creation of an 'alternative state' as part of the struggle. This idea was to be discounted as impractical, but Sinn Féin's Tom Hartely was to be charged later when found with some documents relating to it in his possession.

Adams began to reread and study the writings of the heroes of Irish republicanism, such as James Connolly, Padraic Pearse, James Fintan Lalor and Liam Mellows. It was arranged that the inmates of Cage 11 would give up their parcels for a few weeks so that instead they could have books sent in from the Connolly Association in London.

Adams also began to write. His 'Brownie' columns began to appear in the *Republican News*, a Northern Ireland Sinn Féin publication whose editor had recently been replaced by Belfast republicans Danny Morrison and Tom Hartley, men who held similar views to Adams. He wrote some educational material, a pamphlet entitled *Peace in Ireland*, and a book, *Our British Problem*. The book had two parts: one was a consideration of the issues in Northern Ireland and the republican struggle, and the second offered an alternative structure for Ireland. Although the book was never published, some of the ideas in it were to form the basis of a number of changes in Sinn Féin's policy over the following decade.

The pamphlet, *Peace in Ireland*, was written as a result of the death of former Cage 11 comrade, 23-year-old Danny Lennon, who had finished his sentence and been released. On the afternoon of 10 August 1976, Lennon was driving a car with a dismantled rifle hidden in the back seat when he was spotted and chased by a British army convoy through Andersonstown. The soldiers opened fire and shot Lennon dead at the wheel of his car, which careered off the road and crashed into Anne Maguire and her four children as they walked along the pavement. Mrs Maguire was badly injured and three of her children were killed. (Mrs Maguire was to later claim that her children had been killed by British Army bullets before the car hit them. She later killed herself.) Anne Maguire's sister, Mairéad Corrigan, broke down weeping on the television news that night. She was later contacted by a viewer, Betty Williams, another Belfast Catholic, and together with *Irish Press* journalist Ciaran McKeown, they founded the Peace Movement. Within weeks marches of tens of thousands of people, including outraged Protestants, were taking place north and south of the border, in an emotional appeal for an end to the violence.

Adams wrote his pamphlet in September 1976. Subtitled *A Broad Analysis of the Present Situation*, he argued that the root cause of the violence was the political regimes, both north and south: 'The system the Irish live under is not built for peace, because neither the Stormont or Leinster House regimes are capable of running peaceful societies.' He described the poverty in Ballymurphy and claimed that the peaceful demands of the community there could not be met by Stormont, because of its sectarian nature. Even with Stormont gone, it was not in the nature of the existing political regimes to be able to concede to these demands. In these circumstances, some opted for revolutionary violence as the only way of changing the system.

And in an article titled 'In Defence of Danny Lennon', published in *An Phoblacht*, Adams wrote that Lennon was a 'second timer', i.e. that he had returned to the IRA after being released from prison and had 'spent his last few months in this cage'. Lennon knew what the struggle was about, wrote Adams. 'His death was a contradiction of the life he had spent, fighting for young children such as they' [the Maguire children]. 'Jesus have pity. None of us stands guiltless.'

The prison years for Adams, in a way, came at an opportune time. The defects in the structure of the whole republican movement were becoming evident during those years, most especially during the extended cease-fire of 1975, which as it progressed caused increasing damage to the republican movement, yet was not ended for eighteen months. Also, the fighting had gone on long enough to allow the organisation to assess its deficiencies and to begin to change organically. The practice of being at war was showing up the weaknesses of the IRA. Adams was in a position to be able to consider these issues in the relative quiet of Long Kesh. The camp contained republicans both old and young, urban and rural, experienced and inexperienced. It was the perfect, and perhaps the only possible, assembly point for exchanging such divergent views and discussing changes that might be needed.

Ulsterisation, Criminalisation and Normalisation

The June 1973 elections to the new Northern Ireland Assembly led to the SDLP winning nineteen seats and Brian Faulkner's Official Unionists winning twenty-four. Together with the Alliance Party, they began to discuss the make-up of the new executive, the final details of which were to be worked out in the Sunningdale conference, attended by the representatives of the British and Irish governments. This political initiative by Whitelaw was opposed by the IRA, who feared it would allow the SDLP win increasing support among the nationalist population and make way for the establishment of an internal solution to Northern Ireland's problems.

Just five weeks after the new Assembly's executive took office on 1 January 1974, the British Prime Minister, Edward Heath, who had been battling a miners' strike at home, called a general election. The poll, on 28 February, saw the anti-Assembly parties, who had collected under the United Ulster Unionist Coalition, win fifty-one per cent of the votes, and eleven of the twelve Northern Ireland seats at Westminster. An umbrella group sheltering unionist politicians, trade unionists and paramilitaries launched a campaign to have the Sunningdale Agreement, and specifically the Council of Ireland, abolished, and demanded new elections for the Assembly. The protest, a general strike, began on 15 May and by 20 May Northern Ireland was at a standstill, with the power grid closed down, and the following day an announcement was made that an embargo on petrol and oil was to begin. The action, which was a mix of genuine protest and intimidation, was a success. Faulkner and the rest of the executive resigned on 28 May. The next day the general strike was called off.

Merlyn Rees had been appointed the new Secretary of State for Northern Ireland by Harold Wilson's incoming Labour government, and he continued with the new British strategy aimed at bringing peace to the six counties. It was recognised that the purely military attempt to subdue the IRA, which had been pursued in the early '70s, had failed and that the existence of internment and special-catagory status in the prisons were bad for Britain's image abroad. Soundings began between the new Secretary of State and the Provisionals about the possibility of a cease-fire and the arrangement of talks. According to his own account, Rees had no intention of meeting the Provos, (the 1972 meeting was now perceived as a mistake), but he did wish for a drop in the level of violence, something which he hoped would allow him to press for some sort of acceptable political machinery to be set up in Northern Ireland.[2]

A Commons announcement made known to the Provisionals what was on offer if they ceased hostilities, with the list of items including the phasing out of internment and an end to the signing of interim custody orders (which allowed for detention without trial). On 9 February 1975 the IRA announced that hostilities against the British forces would cease from 6pm on 10 February. Incident centres were to be set up in the Catholic ghettos and the British authorities would liaise through them with republican representatives of the nationalist community.

The 'cease-fire' proved to be almost fatal to the Provisional IRA, and took place during a year that saw a shocking level of tit for tat sectarian killing. It was felt by some in the movement that the leadership had lost direction.

At one point during this period the IRA in Belfast was considering a 'helicopter escape' to pull Adams and Bell from the clutches of the Maze (formerly Long Kesh), but it was decided not to go ahead with the scheme. Sometime earlier leading Provisional Seamus Twomey had been rescued from Mountjoy Prison in Dublin, when he was lifted from an exercise yard by an IRA-commandeered helicopter.

Adams was later to say that in the years 1974 to 1976 the British government created an atmosphere which had led to the belief that they were considering withdrawal. In this situation, the IRA had called a 'limited bilateral truce to give the British Government room to consider the republican position'. This wind-down of the IRA's armed struggle had allowed the British to introduce criminalisation against the most confused background possible. They were able to withdraw some regular army units, transfer more duties to the RUC and UDR and 'probably came as near at that time to defeating the republican struggle than at any time during the last [twenty] years'.[3]

As well as the measures recommended in the Diplock Report, Rees was also working on the introduction of elements of the Gardiner Report, which had been published on 31 January 1975. This report, which followed an investigation of the operation of the Emergency Provisions Act in Northern Ireland, stated that it considered the granting of special-catagory status to convicted prisoners, which Adams had discussed with British officials in a country-house in Derry in 1972, a mistake. From 1 March 1976 all convicted prisoners were to be treated the same as any other prisoner in the United Kingdom, they decided. (New cell blocks, more appropriate to the containment of ordinary criminals, had been under construction since 1973. Their shape was to lead to their later being dubbed the H-Blocks.) The authorities intended to replace the existing legislation, used to intern or detain suspected paramilitaries without trial, with new criminal legislation and court procedures which would allow them claim that IRA prisoners were ordinary convicted murderers, thieves and kidnappers – i.e. common criminals.

After the introduction of the Emergency Provisions Act in 1973, extensive intelligence screening, in-depth interrogation, house searches and frequent arrests for questioning began, all aimed at gathering intelligence and discouraging involvement with the republican movement. In 1973, the peak year for house searches, 74,556 searches were carried out. With most of the searches taking place in nationalist areas, and the number of houses searched equal to nearly one-fifth of all the homes in the six counties, this led to a massive resentment of the army among nationalists and increased support or understanding for the IRA. This war of political suppression, with the British army playing a leading role, was to be ended with the introduction of the recommendations in the Gardiner and Diplock Reports.

The British strategies were given the names 'Ulsterisation, Criminalisation and Normalisation'. By replacing the army in the front line with members of the RUC and the UDR, the perception of the conflict could be changed from one of Irish republicans versus the British to one of republicans versus the police and local defence force of the six counties. The RUC developed even further into a police force which resembled an army in a country experiencing extensive civil unrest. By getting rid of special-catagory status in the prisons, convicted paramilitaries could be classified as criminals and the acts they carried out classified as criminal acts. The IRA would be denied the opportunity to call their campaign a political struggle.

However, in order to allow the authorities deal with the extraordinary security situation which existed in Northern Ireland, they were forced to introduce drastic changes to the criminal law, including extended periods of detention and convictions in Diplock courts based solely on the evidence of men who turned Queen's evidence after being offered immunity for their own crimes, or on 'confessions' signed in unsatisfactory circumstances. The interrogation centres at Castlereagh and Gough Barracks began to earn a notorious reputation in this regard. By 1977 the then Secretary of State, Roy Mason, believed they had the situation in Northern Ireland under control, but a British army report a year later was of the opinion that one element of British strategy, the military suppression of persistent resistance would be impossible.[4] A critical element of the criminalisation policy – the ending of special-catagory status in the prisons – was also to prove impossible, but the British were not to learn this for another three years.

The Brownie Column

The first of Adams' columns written from Long Kesh under the pen-name 'Brownie' appeared in the *Republican News* of 16 August 1975. Though it stated that he had been asked to jot down bits and pieces about life in the camp, the column was to regularly stray from that brief over the next 19 months and consider numerous aspects of the IRA campaign and politics in Ireland on both sides of the border.

In his first piece he painted a pen-picture of life in the camp, expressing the hope that the rumoured recent killing in Belfast was not another sectarian death. (There were a large number of tit for tat sectarian killings during the long truce in the mid-'70s.) Sectarian killings, he wrote, help only the British, letting them 'get on with making profits' as the Catholic and Protestant people of Northern Ireland fight among themselves.

His second piece did not appear until 11 October and after a consideration of the problem of early and late risers in the huts, mentioned the suggestion by Rees that the speed of the release of detainees was linked to everyone 'being good'. (The detainees were being released on a gradual basis as the truce continued.) Adams wrote that 'the war' began with the British presence, not with the introduction of internment, and that it would continue as long as the British presence remained. He also took up the subject of learning the Irish language – a project he was then involved in himself – writing that there was more to freedom than British withdrawal. 'Without our own language, we will be building on sand,' he wrote.

In his third piece entitled 'Active Abstentionism', Adams considered the building of an alternative administration in areas with strong republican support. He agreed completely with abstentionism from the 'British established and orientated partitionist assemblies', but then went on to write that abstentionism could be a more positive and living weapon. While having no doubt that abstentionism as it was then practised did work against British efforts – because as long as republicans refused to take part in any effort at a solution the British would not succeed – he went on to say that if republicans were going to create such a vacuum, then the people were going to vote for the SDLP. The republicans should thus fill any vacuum they created with efforts which lay 'outside the British solution'. What was needed, he said, was an alternative to the British and 'Free State' administrations in Ireland. Why not cement the control which republicans had in Northern Ireland's nationalist areas into a local government structure, the lowest and most important element of the Dáil Uladh (the parliament for the nine counties of Ulster proposed for the federal Ireland envisaged in Sinn Féin policy at the time). Adams supported his idea by saying that it was not the violence of 1969 which most upset the British, but the active abstention which existed in some areas where communities had retreated behind the barricades. However, he emphasised that he was not advocating any diversion from the war effort. 'Far from it!' he wrote. 'I'm advocating an extension of it, plus an implementation of policy.'

The idea was returned to in a piece published a month later. Again it was pointed out that it was not an argument for a de-escalation of military activity and that it had its roots in radical republicanism. The IRA was not just looking for a 'Britless Ireland', but for a socialist republic, he wrote. What he was advocating was the complete fusion of the military and political strategies. 'If we have only the local unit in an area, then the Brit wins by isolating or removing that unit from the people. If that unit is part of an aggressive or peoples' resistance structure, the Brit must remove everyone concerned, from school children to customers in the coops, from paper-sellers to street committees, before he can defeat us. Immersed in the structure as part of the alternative, republicanism cannot be isolated and will never be defeated.' He quoted one of his favourite republicans from the beginning of the century, Liam Mellows: 'An object, a target, must be presented for the enemy to hit at. Otherwise it becomes a fight, apparently, between individuals.' Adams then continued, 'The building of a national alternative to Free State and Brit institutions can, and must, start now'.

He considered the idea again a few months later and wrote about how the IRA should replace structures destroyed by the war campaign, such as replacing the bus service with the peoples' taxis or the routed police with peoples' militias, and how these alternatives could be used as part of the struggle. He repeats his point about how this makes it more difficult for the British to isolate the IRA from its support base: 'Comrades, this is necessary work. It cannot be left to Sinn Féin, the leadership, or anyone else.'

The idea of an alternative system of local government was to be abandoned, but the Provisionals were to get involved in 'community policing', some commercial activities and in organising a local postal service in some parts of Belfast. But while the idea of an alternative administration was to be dropped, fundamental ideas behind the strategy were retained and subsequently were to play an important role in the development of Sinn Féin policy.

In another of his pieces Adams wrote about the need for physical force as an element of 'active republicanism'. There had to be fighting because the enemy allowed no other choice: 'It's hard for me to write that down because God knows, maybe I won't fight again and it will be cast up at me, but still it needs to be said, even by a coward like myself, because at least I will move aside for the fighters,' he wrote self-deprecatingly. However, he continued, the people they were fighting for were all around them now and must be carried with them, otherwise the 'Republic' they were fighting for would be all the weaker. Commitment to republicanism must not be restricted to honouring fallen dead who had sacrificed their lives.

He addressed the issue in a more personal way in the following week's piece: 'I firmly believe that the course of action I take, rightly or wrongly, is the only one open to me, because those who have a vested interest in me leave me no choice. The course I take involves the use of physical force, but only if I achieve the situation where my people genuinely prosper can my course of action be seen, by me, to have been justified. In taking this action, I have also taken certain risks. I have to accept those risks. They are a consequence of my actions and I cannot complain if I am hurt, if I am killed, or if I am imprisoned.' He went on to say that 'at least' he had had some freedom of choice in the matter, not like the victim of the sectarian killing or a civilian casualty. Others that have used their freedom of choice to take a side in the battle, like the prison officers, must also like him be prepared to take the risks which are a consequence of that choice. In a section expressing doubt, he wrote, 'Maybe in ten years time if all this has achieved nothing, I'll wonder why I wrote all this and why I thought like this'.[5]

In his writings 'Brownie' also addressed current political developments. Looking at the 'Free State' he wrote that in the past the Dublin government had said that the IRA impeded their efforts to unite Ireland, but now that government had plainly shown its true, anti-republican colours. 'As I see it we need to expand our struggle onto a 32 country basis,' he wrote, and called for agitation on local issues in the twenty-six counties.

In a subsequent article he wrote about Merlyn Rees putting the RUC into the front line and stated that Ulsterisation must be resisted 'at all costs'.

As the policy of Ulsterisation continued, he wrote a piece in August 1976, entitled 'Beir Bua Againn' ('We will win'), in which he addressed the issue of IRA operations. 'Ultimately I see the defeat of the IRA as the rejection of the IRA by the people... Without their support we are only of nuisance value and of no great danger or threat to British interests.' The British were determined to defeat the IRA and so, following on the logic of his position on the only possible way the IRA could be defeated, he wrote, 'We must employ tactics that have the maximum effect on the establishment with the minimum risk to ourselves and our support'. He called for constant review and assessment of the movement and its objectives. Objectives had to be agreed on before it was possible to agree on the means to achieve those objectives. Anyone who did not fully understand and support those objectives and means would not be allowed to influence policy.

During his time writing the 'Brownie' columns Adams repeatedly referred to the Irish republican writers of the early twentieth century, with lengthy quotes from Connolly, Mellows, Lalor and Pearse. In one such piece, he quotes Lalor advising that it is easy to identify your enemy. He is the one who objects to every plan of armed resistance that is proposed, yet he produces no better proposal of his own.

Some of the column space was used to swipe at the administrations on both sides of the border. In a piece called 'Terrorism' he wrote about the extensive powers given to the state under the 1973 Emergency Provisions Act and asked, 'Will the real terrorists please stand?' In another, he argued that Articles 1 and 2 of the 1937 Constitution of the Irish Republic, which at once refused to recognise the border and at the same time stated that the provisions of the Constitution applied only to the twenty-six counties, allowed de Valera to lead Irish nationalism down 'a cul-de-sac'. He wrote about the failure of the twenty-six-county economy and asked whether the introduction of the State of Emergency legislation by the Dublin government might be due in part to their wishing to deflect attention away from the consequences of this failure.

In the 19 February 1977 issue of *Republican News* 'Brownie' announced his imminent release and described how he was looking forward to seeing his son, who was born after he had been picked up in July 1973.

7: The Birth of Sinn Féin

Around the time of Adams' release from the Maze in early 1977 there began what an IRA spokesman was to later describe as 'a reappraisal of the struggle by the entire republican movement'.[1] During 1977 and '78 an in-depth study of the aims and strategy of the movement led it to adopt a number of basic principles and objectives from which grew the later direction of Sinn Féin and the IRA.

The new ideas strongly resembled those which had been developed in Cage 11 of Long Kesh by Adams and his comrades. It was decided there was a need to build a political party and a thirty-two-county struggle. This was the most important of the new decisions on fundamental policy and it involved an almost complete reversal for the Provisionals. There needed to be a popularisation of the struggle, of which armed conflict was only a part. The struggle should be developed on economic, social and cultural issues, with a return to the radical roots of republicanism. There would be a positive attitude towards using elections for propaganda purposes. Electoralism was a tactic. Armed struggle was a tactic. There was also a need to structure the support base.

Sinn Féin at the time was only a protest and support organisation, but it had a membership and structure which could be worked on and developed into a political party. These new positions were taken up by Sinn Féin's central executive, the Ard Comhairle, as the years progressed. At first Adams was a lone voice on the executive, but as the force of the ideas made their impact they were accepted and the number of young northerners such as Morrison, McGuinness and Hartely on the Ard Comhairle began to increase.

During Adams' prison years a commission set up inside Long Kesh considered the existing structure of the IRA and developed a new structure aimed at countering inroads being made by British and RUC intelligence work and at fitting in better with the needs of the changing republican movement. A copy of the report outlining this new structure was found during a Garda search of a flat occupied by Seamus Twomey in December 1977. It showed how the British were having some success in the fight against the IRA and also revealed the relationship that existed between the IRA and Sinn Féin. The document read:

Staff report: The three-day and seven-day detention orders are breaking volunteers, and it is the Irish Republican Army's own fault for not indoctrinating volunteers with the psychological strength to resist interrogation. Coupled with this factor, which is contributing to our defeat, we are burdened with an inefficient infrastructure of commands, brigades, battalions and companies. The old system with which Brits and Branch are familiar has to be changed. We recommend reorganisation and remotivation, the building of a new Irish Republican Army.

We emphasise a return to secrecy and strict discipline. Army men must be in total control of all sections of the movement.

1. A new rank of Education Officer must be created. GHQ must have a department of Education Officers available for lectures and discussions at weapons training camps. Anti-interrogation lectures must be given in conjunction with indoctrination lectures. The ideal outcome is that no volunteer should be charged unless caught red-handed. It should be pointed out to new recruits the failures of our past structures – the number of men who have been arrested and signed their freedom away. The commonsense methods of personal security should be thrashed out. Any new recruit mixing with known volunteers should be suspended pending discipline. We must gear ourselves towards long term armed struggle based on putting unknown men and new recruits into a new structure. The new structure shall be a cell system.

2. Ideally a cell should consist of four people. Rural areas we decided, should be treated as separate cases to that of a city and town brigade/ command. For this reason our proposals will affect mainly city and town areas where the majority of our operations are carried out and where the biggest proportion of our support lies anyway.

As we have already said, all new recruits are to be passed into a cell structure. Existing battalion and company staffs must be dissolved over a period of months with present brigades then deciding who passes into the reorganised cell structure and who goes into the brigade controlled and compartmentalised civil administration (explained later). The cells of four volunteers will be controlled militarily by the brigade's/command's intelligence officer. Cells will be financed through their cell leader who will be funded through the OC co-ordinator. That is, for wages, for running costs, financing of operations. (Expenses, etc will be dealt with through the OC.) Cells must be specialised into IC cells, sniping cells, execution, bombing, robberies, etc. The cell will have no control of weapons or explosives, but should be capable of dumping weapons overnight (in the case of a postponed operation). The weapons and explosives should be under the complete control of the brigade's/

command's QM and EO respectively. Cells should operate as often as possible outside of their own areas; both to confuse Brit intelligence (which would thus increase our security) and to expand our operational areas. Brigades must be made use of in all operations.

The breaking up of the present structure into administration sections and operational cells will make for maximum military effectiveness, greater security, a more efficient back-up structure to increase support and cater for our people's problems. Thus our operations officer can go straight into an area and deal exclusively with military operations and problems.

All present volunteers under the old structure must be reeducated and given up-dated lectures in combating new interrogation techniques...

Sinn Féin should come under army organisers at all levels. Sinn Féin should employ full-time organisers in big republican areas. Sinn Féin should be radicalised (under army direction) and should agitate about social and economic issues which attack the welfare of the people. Sinn Féin should be directed to infiltrate other organisations to win support for, and sympathy to, the movement. Sinn Féin should be reeducated and have a big role to play in publicity and propaganda depts, complaints and problems (making no room for RUC opportunism). It gains the respect of the people which in turn leads to increased support for the cell.

The Way Forward

The first phase of the Provisional IRA's battle to drive the British out of Northern Ireland by the use of force had almost ended with the defeat of the IRA. The cease-fire, which had begun in February 1975 and had lasted for eighteen months, had come close to dealing a terminal blow to the movement. Now there was to be a complete and badly needed overhaul. The significant proportion of the nationalist community which had been behind the IRA in the early years had been whittled down, both as a result of war-weariness and dislike of the viciousness of the IRA campaign.

The membership of the IRA itself was tired and finding it impossible to keep up the momentum which it felt was necessary to push the British out. When the ceasefire was announced, there was little for the IRA to do. When there was no fighting, there was little reason for the IRA's existence – there was no struggle.

During 1975 – a particularly horrific year in Northern Ireland, with a death toll of 247 by the year's end – many of the killings were tit for tat sectarian murders carried out by IRA and loyalist paramilitaries. (During that year, Adams sent a letter out to the Belfast Brigade from Long Kesh, asking what was going on. He and other volunteers in the camp were worried that the sectarian killings would be used by the British in anti-IRA propaganda, painting them as blood-thirsty sectarian bigots and gangsters.)

When the Provisionals formed after the split in the IRA during 1969-'70, the nature of the dispute that caused the schism led to the creation of a grouping which was strongly in favour of militarism and almost totally devoid of any political content. In fact, politics was considered by many to be something which should be avoided, as it had always led to weakness and thereby endangered the war effort and the community which the IRA was pledged to protect. The massive destruction and carnage which the Provisionals had caused in Northern Ireland and Britain had failed to force the British to leave. But it was necessary that volunteers continue to believe that their efforts, and the sacrifices of those who had died or were imprisoned, had not been in vain. It was also necessary that they believe the British were on the verge of giving in, that victory was imminent.

In 1972 Adams had voiced the opinion that victory was probably some way off and that things would get worse before they got better. He was reprimanded for daring to suggest such a thing. But by the mid-'70s, six to seven years into the campaign, far from looking like leaving, the British looked like they were winning.

It was the first time that the IRA had fought a continual campaign for so many years and this allowed the movement to contemplate developments which it otherwise might not have been able to and also, to an extent, forced changes in the movement. Adams, in prison and later when released, was at the heart of analysing the faults of the movement and drafting the blueprint which would make it more resilient.

There is an inherent strain in fighting a long-term revolutionary campaign and looking for support from the people. The growth of a structured support base is often inhibited by the actions of the militants, and most especially by the blunders, or planned operations, which lead to the deaths of civilians. Ulsterisation (the replacement of the British soldiers with security force members who were almost entirely from the Protestant community in Northern Ireland) changed the public perception of the fighting and helped the British argue it was sectarian. Adams was totally behind the use of violence, but he gave it a new purpose. It was 'armed propaganda', a way of keeping the issue of Northern Ireland in the news, of maintaining pressure on the political situation and of bringing to an end any political solutions which in the republican view would be a betrayal of the fight for national self-determination.

There was a need to be pragmatic about everything, he reasoned, and it was wrong to hold any tenets of republican policy as beyond rejection. If violence was armed propaganda, then acts of violence which led to a serious damaging of the support base were obviously bad acts. Not only did they work against the task of winning votes – which the republicans could point to in support of their argument that their's was a political struggle and not gangsterism and that they represented somebody – but such acts also gave the British useful propaganda to use against them. The fighting needed to be tuned, to allow maximum growth of support while still keeping up the pressure and keeping the guerrilla army operative.

Adams emerged from Long Kesh to take up a powerful position in the republican movement. The stock of the old leadership was about to begin its descent, with the length of the ceasefire in 1975 being seen as an almost fatal mistake in judgment. *The Republican News*, edited by Morrison and Hartley, had begun to push the new line and to diverge in view from the Dublin-based official organ of the movement, *An Phoblacht*. The young northern republicans who had grown up with the struggle and with the injustices in Northern Ireland were beginning to win more power on the Army Council and in their efforts to change the movement's philosophy, the logic of their arguments was undermining the position of the leadership, whether that was their intention or not.

Adams wanted to publicise the new analysis of 'the way forward'. It was time to build those aspects of the movement which had been lost following the split with the Officials (who had gone on to evolve into the Workers' Party) and, as Adams saw it, reap the benefits of a lot of the political work which had been done in the 1960s. Now it was time for the Provisionals to join the vanguard of anti-imperialism, north and south of the border. He wanted to introduce republicans to a more sophisticated struggle, not just a militant 'Brits-out' one, but a campaign to rout British control in its many forms from the entire island. He hoped that while helping to put the struggle on this new and more sophisticated basis, he might at the same time reinvigorate the movement, which had grown somewhat disheartened.

The chosen time and place for outlining this new political analysis and for rejecting the view that British withdrawal was soon to come was at the annual speech at the Wolfe Tone memorial in Co. Kildare. Adams and a number of others worked long and hard on the wording of the address (Adams had done some of this work while still in Long Kesh) and it was delivered by veteran northern republican Jimmy Drumm on 12 June 1977.

The British, the assembled crowd was told, were not about to leave; in fact, they were intent on stabilising the North. The war of liberation could not be fought successfully 'on the backs of the oppressed in the six counties, nor around the physical presence of the British army'. Socialist republicans had been isolated around the armed struggle and this was dangerous. They were calling for the development of a strong political movement in the entire island, committed to anti-imperialism. Republicans were to forge links with the workers and radical trade unionists, to create an irrepressible mass movement which would ensure mass support for the continuing armed struggle in the six counties and make for a competent force in the event of a serious conflict. In many ways, this thinking was a return to that of the socialists who had led the IRA in the late '60s. The difference, however, was that this time an active and strong military campaign was being fought and was to be maintained.

Prison Again

In December 1977, the IRA captured and killed a British soldier, Paul Harman, whom they said they had caught engaged in 'SAS-type activities' in West Belfast under the name of Hughill. Harman had with him miniaturised photographs of seventy-three republicans, with a picture of Adams among them. Around his picture and that of another man and a woman were pencilled circles. Sinn Féin alleged that Harman was an intelligence officer involved in planning assassination attempts.

If the British were trying to kill Adams, it was evidence of their awareness of his growing importance within the republican movement. By the end of 1976 the military control of the organisation had all but been taken off the old southern-based leadership. The units from Northern Ireland set themselves up as a virtually autonomous Northern Command. Adams, having worked on the new structure and policy for the movement while in prison, came out to take a prominent role in the reorganisation, and in the movement itself. Still only twenty-seven years old, he was well on the way to being recognised as a leader of the republican movement.

He was appointed publicity director of Sinn Féin following his release and at the Ard Fheis that year was appointed to the Ard Comhairle, where he began to press for the changes which he and his northern colleagues felt were needed. But then a particularly ghastly incident in the litany of horrors which were being inflicted on the people of Ireland occurred.

On the evening of 17 February 1978 a bomb was placed at the window of a hotel by an IRA unit who then made their escape by car. The first telephone they stopped at to deliver their warning turned out to be broken, and they had to drive on in search of another. Eventually a telephone warning was made to the GPO. The call was received at 8.57pm. Immediately the RUC were informed and units raced towards the La Mon Hotel, Co. Down. A call was made ahead to warn those in the hotel of the danger but the man who answered the call said there had already been an explosion, and that ambulances were needed quickly. It later emerged that the bomb had exploded just as the call was being received at the GPO.

The bomb itself had been quite small, but two canisters of petrol were attached to it, with sugar or some such substance mixed through it. When the burning fuel was sent flying through the hotel, the mixture stuck to whatever, or whoever, it fell on. Mary Rainey (25) was sitting at the top table of the Peacock Room where a function was underway, 'I remember a blast and my plate jumping towards my head as the whole table fell. Something hit my back'. She saw a stream of petrol run down the middle of the room 'and then a sheet of flame shot up. We were at the top table and were able to get out. The others were not'.

A man told afterwards of trying to rub the sticky blazing substance off his hands but not being able to. 'A lot of people were trying to stop themselves burning but you just couldn't get rid of it,' he said. A woman had been seen trapped under a table and people tried to save her. But then the tar from the melting ceiling began to fall into the burning room and she had to be abandoned. Seven men and five women died in the blast and the ensuing blaze; many more were injured, some of them horribly burned. Small pieces of charred remains made people believe at first that children were among the dead. On the night of the attack there were 700 people in the hotel, many of them children. Two functions were going on – the annual dinner of the Junior Motorcycle Club and a function for the Irish Collie Dog Club. When the fire died down, dogs' paws were found among the charred wreckage.

It was late that night when Gerry Adams heard of the disaster at La Mon. He was in the house on Harrowgate Street in the Beechmount area where he had been arrested back in March 1972. (He, Colette and their child Gearóid had since moved into the house.) The news mesmerised and demoralised him to such an extent that rather than do as he should and go to a safe house where the security forces could not find him, he stayed at his family home. Early the next day, the house was raided. He was arrested and once again taken to Castlereagh. There was widespread disgust and outrage at the bombing and unionist politicians were calling for a clamp-down on the IRA and the arrest of its leaders. Adams was kept at Castlereagh for seven days and during questioning was shown gruesome pictures of the burnt victims of the bombing. While some of his interrogators tried to scare him with threats and intimidation, others hardly bothered to question him at all, but instead played cards during their periods with him. One officer tried to convince Adams of the evil of what he was involved in and used quotes from the Bible to reinforce his argument. There was no violence. The police took his clothes and gave him a jumpsuit to wear, but he refused to put it on. He asked to see his doctor as was his right, and when the doctor came he went to see him naked. The police, embarrassed, returned his clothes.

The cells in Castlereagh are completely insulated. Not a sound penetrates from outside. The white light in the white room is left on constantly. There is a bed, with paper sheets. In all, the cells have a disconcerting effect on the people being kept there. Adams was kept for the full seven-day period, then he was charged with membership of the IRA and moved to Crumlin Road Prison in Belfast to be held on remand.

Political status for prisoners had been removed in 1976 as part of the criminalisation policy and Adams was apprehensive about what would be his first experience of prison under the new rules. As a remand prisoner, he was allowed to keep his own clothes and so did not get involved in the dispute over the wearing of prison uniforms. Inside the prison, an old Victorian building which was grossly overcrowded, the authorities had – political status or not – decided to group all the republican prisoners in one area and the loyalists in another. There was an hour's exercise every 24 hours, but as the republican and loyalist prisoners were in the same wing, away from the 'ordinary criminals', they took their exercise in turns, which meant the inmates had only one hour every 48 hours.

Adams was put in a cell with two young republicans who liked to play pop music until early in the morning. The atmosphere in the prison was different again from that in the detainees' or sentenced prisoners' cages in Long Kesh. Most inmates were waiting around for their trial and sentences before being moved to the H-Blocks. (Adams met a colleague one day who had been in Long Kesh with him as they crossed a yard in opposite directions. 'I only got life,' the prisoner shouted happily, glad he had not been given a recommended sentence for an even longer period.) During his stay at Crumlin Road there was a major clamp-down on Sinn Féin, initiated by Roy Mason, which led to a large influx of Belfast's more prominent Sinn Féin activists into the prison.

Later, Adams was moved up to Long Kesh (Maze) Prison, where the H-Blocks cells had been built and where the no-wash and blanket protests had begun the year before, in protest against the loss of special-category status. (The prisoners had refused to wear the prescribed prison uniform.) Once again, he began to file complaints against the way in which the Northern Ireland Office was running its prisons. The senior prison officer from Long Kesh, Davey Long, had been moved to the H-Blocks and Adams found himself again making complaints to the man about inadequate supplies and other issues. Again, Adams was allowed to keep his own clothes, so he did not join the blanket protest. He 'slopped out' while there, but joined in the no-wash protest and refused to clean his cell. He also discovered that the genesis of the so-called 'dirty protest' was not a planned escalation of the political protest by the prisoners, as was believed outside, but was actually due to the prisoners not being given enough time to slop out by the prison officers.

As a high security prisoner, Adams was put in a cell on his own. The atmosphere in the blocks was tense, with the prisoners, most of whom were quite young, standing up to the prison authorities even though they were isolated in pairs in their cells. They would shout back and forth to each other in an attempt to maintain morale. For his visits, Adams was brought to a special section of the complex and there he got to meet and speak with some of the blanket men. Although they were wearing prison uniforms when he met them – for the purpose of receiving visitors – they still made for a bizarre sight, with laceless boots, scruffy, ill-fitting clothes, long hair and unkempt beards. Some were men he had known from Long Kesh's Cage 11.

When Adams was brought to court to be charged on the morning of 25 February, his solicitor Paddy McGrory said Adams had told his interrogators he was revolted by the La Mon bombing. He also told the court his client was considering taking legal action against a number of British newspapers which had claimed he was a senior member of the Belfast IRA. The court charged Adams that from March 1977, when he was released from Long Kesh, to the date of his arrest, he had been a member of the IRA. Following his arrest he had been shown a video of a BBC *Tonight* programme, 'The Republicans', which showed Adams at the 1977 Ard Fheis. It was to be claimed that the wording of the speech he delivered there indicated that he was a member of the IRA. A later bail application was unsuccessful. Three months after his arrest, the period of alleged IRA membership was extended backwards to 1 April 1976, based on the position he took during a Long Kesh parade on that date.

Adams had been one of twenty-one republicans arrested after the La Mon bombing. While he was held on remand, a massive publicity campaign was launched by Sinn Féin, involving tens of thousands of leaflets giving details of the case and alleging political harassment. They were distributed all over West Belfast and the details contained in them were published in *An Phoblacht*. Adams denied the charge of IRA membership. When the trial came to court after eight months, his solicitor argued that there was insufficient evidence to support the charge. The judge agreed and the case was thrown out.

He was released in time for the 1978 Ard Fheis where he was elected Vice President of Sinn Féin. Before the meeting he had met with the President, Ruairí Ó Brádaigh, and told him how serious he considered the situation inside the prisons to be and how much he feared the possibility of a crisis. He assisted Ó Brádaigh in drafting a few paragraphs on the issue, to be inserted into his presidential speech.

At the Ard Fheis the Ard Comhairle delivered its decision that Sinn Féin would not contest the 1979 EEC elections as was advocated by some members, but it was decided that the party would contest the local government elections in the Republic, which were due to take place the following year.

A Socialist Republican Party

In June 1979 Adams delivered the annual Bodenstown speech, in which he outlined the broad direction it was felt the movement should go. Republicans were, he said, 'opposed to all forms and manifestations of imperialism and capitalism. We stand for an Ireland free, united, socialist and Gaelic.... Our movement needs constructive and thoughtful self-criticism. We also require links with those oppressed by economic and social pressures. Today's circumstances and our objectives dictate the need for building an

agitational struggle in the counties, an economic resistance movement, lining up republicans with other sections of the working
class. It needs to be done now because to date our most glaring
weakness lies in our failure to develop revolutionary politics and to
build an alternative to so-called constitutional politics'.

The basic attitude of Sinn Féin had been established, but it had
yet to work out how exactly to put these ideas into practice.
However, all this 'politics' was upsetting to some of the membership and among the more conservative elements, as well as among
some of the traditional Catholic element, there was disquiet about
the left-wing rhetoric. The left-wing talk, the efforts to cultivate
links with trade unionists and other groups, bore a striking resemblance to the rhetoric of the leadership in the '60s. The mur-
murings of disquiet also had something of a familiar ring. At a
Pearse Centenary meeting in Monaghan in September, Adams said
the republican movement was 'striving for a thirty-two-county
democratic socialist republic and we are not ashamed of it'. Allegations about the party adopting Marxist policies were also causing
worry in the ranks of the supporters in the US. A month later
Adams was questioned about this in an interview and denied that
Sinn Féin was a now a Marxist organisation.[2] Asked had the party
not swung to the left in recent years, he replied that the 1916
Proclamation was a radical document. The party believed in decentralised socialism and decentralised government structures. It
was a socialist republican or radical republican party, he said.

The objective of that socialist republican party was a thirty-two-
county socialist republic with a strong Gaelic culture. In *An
Phoblacht*, April 1980, Adams wrote an article titled 'Scenario for
Establishing a Socialist Republic', where he divided the 'struggle'
into a number of phases. In phase four, on national elections –
which would come after a British withdrawal from Northern
Ireland – he wrote: 'If feasible at all [national elections] as a way of
providing the means by which socialism can be established, [are]
only viable from a republican position if those representing such a
radical republican movement as envisaged here, secure majority
support in Government'. This position would seem to be one of a
very qualified commitment to constitutional democracy in a thirty-
two-county Ireland. However on numerous other occasions
Adams did emphasise that the justification for the role of the IRA
came from the presence of the British in Northern Ireland, and that
militarism would have no role to play in a thirty-two-county
situation.

8: Prisoners-of-War

When Gerry Adams was released in 1978 after eight months on remand on the IRA membership charge he threw himself back into the work of building a new, more sophisticated movement, a new struggle. He also began to devote a considerable part of his energies to the prison issue. His time in the H-Blocks impressed on him the importance to the movement of the issues being fought out there and their potential for crisis. British strategy was to 'Ulsterise' and 'Normalise' the situation in Northern Ireland, but in order to do that they had to be able to portray the republican prisoners as criminals. By the late 70s the effort to implement this policy was being prevented only by the stubborn inmates in the Maze Prison. The most important front in the battle between the British and the republicans over the criminalisation issue was now within the prisoners' cells.

Sinn Féin's Prisoner-of-War department was rejuvenated and a series of conferences was organised on the prison issue. A POW committee was set up, with Adams one of its members. In September 1979 a conference, chaired by Adams and Joe Cahill, was held in Dublin. In his opening speech Adams explained that they were there to 'assess and invigorate the party's work on behalf of the prisoners'.

The H-Block issue was recognised as the one central to the criminalisation attempt by the British, while another speaker said that 'if the H-Blocks struggle is lost, then there is not much hope of sustaining the present war'.[1] The conference ended with Adams addressing the issue of the 'way forward', in particular the need to mobilise support for the issue: 'The case needs urgent attention. We do not want the kind of situation arising where blanket men might begin to get into the frame of mind that Frank Stagg [an IRA member who had died on hunger-strike] got into. This is something that has to be avoided'.

A 'Smash H-Block' Committee, to be formed the following month in Belfast, was to be open to people who did not support the IRA. The intention was to build an effective, broadly based mass movement which would force the British government to grant political status to republican prisoners.

What Adams had announced was a new departure. Up to then

Sinn Féin had been an organisation isolated in the plethora of political groupings that existed in Northern Ireland. The party had isolated itself by insisting on support for the armed struggle from people and groups it co-operated with and by a desire to be in total control of everything it was involved in. At a conference held in Coalisland in January, a broad range of organisations had gathered to discuss the prison issue, among them the SDLP, People's Democracy, the Communist Party, NICRA, the Association for Legal Justice and a number of community organisations. Sinn Féin also attended, but isolated itself from the proceedings by demanding support for the IRA's campaign.

When the 'Smash H-Block' conference took place in Belfast on Sunday, 26 October, Adams was to tell those present that 'there is a difference between support for the demands of the prisoners and support for the armed struggle'.[2] The republicans were on their way towards extending their field of operation. A committee was elected – with Adams being one of those elected – and there was a provision to co-opt additional members onto it, in order to draw in individuals and groups who had failed to attend the conference. The proposal to set up the committee was drafted by Adams and Hartley. Some groups in attendance wanted a broad anti-imperialist campaign, but Adams called for a single-issue campaign. 'Earlier attempts were made to broaden the campaign. This will not work. If this campaign works, then we can build on our experience,' he said.

Inside the prison hundreds of republican prisoners were involved in the blanket, no-wash and dirty protests – a situation that had grown from the original decision not to wear prison clothing – in their efforts to have political status returned. They spent their days naked, with long lank hair and unkempt beards, in stinking cells caked with their own excreta which they smeared on the walls. On occasion the cells were filled with maggots. Prisoners went through periodic bouts of vomiting. A campaign of assassination had been launched against the prison warders (over a period of four years, eighteen of them were to be killed by the IRA). Tension within the prison was on a knife edge and there was constant beating of the inmates by warders. In the summer of 1978, the Catholic Archbishop of Armagh, Dr Ó Fiaich, visited the H-Blocks and said afterwards that one would hardly allow an animal remain in such conditions – let alone a human being.

'The nearest approach to it that I have seen was the spectacle of hundreds of homeless people living in the sewer pipes in the slums of Calcutta. The stench and filth in some of the cells, with the remains of rotting food and human excreta scattered around the walls was almost unbearable. In two of them I was unable to speak for fear of vomiting,' he said.

The statement by Archbishop Ó Fiaich gave the prisoners a morale boost, as did the high profile which the issue was given in the international media. But there was no indication of a weakening in British resolve. By 1980 the protest had entered its fourth year and there was still no sign of the prisoners achieving their aim. Media interest began to wane and a note of pessimism and desperation developed. The Smash H-Blocks Committee had been successful in bringing attention to the issue, but had failed to make any inroad into British determination to resist.

Within the prison, the discussion turned to the use of the awful weapon of the hunger-strike. The most recent example of its use had been the protest of Frank Stagg in February 1976, when after 60 days of starvation he had died in England's Wakefield Prison. After his death, there was a morbid fight over his emaciated body between republicans and the Irish government, and despite the fact that his body was buried under a concrete slab and given a temporary Garda watch, it was later dug up and reinterred by the IRA, who then fired a shot over the grave. In all, it was an immensely ugly affair.

Some republican members of the H-Block Committee were reporting on the state of mind of the prisoners and their growing conviction of the need to go on hunger-strike. Five demands had been decided on by the prisoners: the right to wear their own clothes, to refuse to do prison work, to receive one parcel per week, to associate freely with one another and the return of remission lost as a result of the protest. A plan for the hunger-strike was drawn up and a large pool of prisoners selected who felt convinced they were willing and had the capacity to starve themselves to death. It was impressed on each candidate that he would not be acting as an individual once he began his strike, but as a representative of all the prisoners. It was decided that seven would go on hunger-strike and that a decision to call it off would have to be taken by all seven and cleared by a committee of Block OCs. There was to be one member from each of the six counties, in order to spread the impact of the drama as widely as possible, and a seventh from the Irish National Liberation Army (INLA).

On the morning of 27 October 1980 the seven hunger-strikers, led by Brendan Hughes, started their fast. On 4 December

Humphrey Atkins, the new Secretary of State, appointed after the 1979 election victory of Margaret Thatcher, announced in the House of Commons that there would be no concessions to the hunger-strikers. However, inside the prison hospital to which the protesters had been removed, a British official was negotiating with the prisoners. On 18 December, as Séan McKenna from Newry was approaching death, the hunger-strike was called off after a vague thirty-four-page document had been drafted as a potential solution to the dispute. But by the end of the following month, it was obvious to the republicans that the document was not going to lead to any of their demands being granted through negotiation. The prisoners felt duped. They were outraged and determined to go straight back on hunger-strike and this time not end until their demands were met.

Hunger-Strike Again

In the smuggled communications between the prisoners and the Army Council, the two sides outlined their views. The prisoners were determined to go on a second hunger-strike, but the Army Council was anxious to avoid another crisis like that created by the first protest. They wrote to the prisoners, pointing out to them that there would be no de-escalation of the war effort as there had been during the first protest. But the prisoners were determined. 'Our decision to hunger strike remains the same,' the camp OC, Bobby Sands, wrote to the Army Council. 'We accept the tragic consequences that must certainly await us and the overshadowing fact that death may not secure a principled settlement.'[3]

The announcement that a second hunger-strike was to begin on 1 March 1981 was made in early February. In the House of Commons Atkins made another statement, proclaiming British government determination not to accede to the prisoners' demands. This time, the hunger-strikers were going to begin their protest one by one, to win maximum effect. The first to start his fast was the former cage-comrade of Adams, the Belfast-born OC in the camp, Bobby Sands, whose twenty-seventh birthday was nine days away. The day he began his fast 3,500 people marched down the Falls Road to mark the event. It was less than half the number that had turned out for a similar march at the beginning of the 1980 protest. Inside the prison, Sands wrote on a piece of toilet paper, 'I am standing on the threshold of another trembling world. May God have mercy on my soul'.[4]

On 15 March Sands was joined on his fast by Francis Hughes, and then later joined by Patsy O'Hara (the INLA OC), Raymond McCreesh and Joe McDonnell. Meanwhile an event had taken place that was to have momentous repercussions not only on the hunger-strike but on the direction that the republican movement was to take in the coming years. The independent republican Westminster MP for Fermanagh/South Tyrone, Frank Maguire, had died of a heart attack on 5 March. The constituency was one in which Adams believed there was a strong case to be made for electoral inter-vention by Sinn Féin. ('Interventions' can occur where candidates are nominated in particular situations where a wave of emotion can be taken advantage of to upset normal voting patterns. 'Electoral strategy' on the other hand is where the party commits itself to the demanding task of beginning the long term enterprise of building an electoral base).

While the Ard Comhairle had decided to adopt a 'positive attitude to elections', this was not known to the bulk of the membership, nor had it been approved of in an Ard Fheis vote. Indeed, at the 1980 Ard Fheis the membership had opted to vote against a proposal to fight local government elections.

Frank Maguire's death and the constituency which he repre-sented caused the same thought to occur in the minds of republi-cans both inside and outside the H-Blocks. Inside the prison it was felt that his death offered a possibility that could not be rejected. The Ard Comhairle met in Dublin shortly after Maguire's death, with the issue of whether or not to contest the by-election the main topic for discussion. Adams put forward the idea that Bobby Sands should go forward for election. He was supported by his co-Vice President, Daithí Ó Connaill. It was agreed that if Maguire's brother Noel and any other nationalist candidate considering contesting the election could be persuaded to leave the field clear for Sands, then his name would be put forward. (Ó Connaill was later to advocate Sands going forward even if he had to compete with another nationalist candidate, but Adams, who did not be-lieve Sands would win if he was not given a clear field, remained convinced of the correctness of the original position.)

A meeting was organised in the Swan Hotel, Monaghan, just south of the border, for republicans from the Fermanagh/South Tyrone constituency. The members voted overwhelmingly against the idea of putting Sands forward. An impromptu meeting of the Ard Comhairle was held afterwards and it was decided to go ahead with Sands' nomination in spite of the vote. Adams called the Belfast HQ and gave instructions for a statement to be issued, with a plea to other possible candidates not to oppose Sands. A local schoolteacher and Sinn Féin activist, Owen Carron, also remained in the hotel afterwards and along with a few colleagues came to the same decision as the Ard Comhairle, that the Sands nomination should go ahead anyway. Adams and others had met with Bernadette McAliskey, the former nationalist MP who was considering standing in the election, and she had agreed to withdraw her nomination to give Sands a clear field. Ó Brádaigh and Ó Connaill had met with Noel Maguire. Adams and Jim Gibney later travelled to Lisnaskea to further press the Sinn Féin case with Maguire, who then told them he would not stand against a prisoner. Meanwhile, the relatives of the hunger-strikers had been lobbying the SDLP not to put anyone forward and, while the party agreed, party member Austin Currie said he would enter his nomination papers if Maguire left the field clear for Sands.

Bobby Sands, MP

On 20 March 1981, with just ten minutes to go to the 4pm deadline, Gerry Adams and Owen Carron stood around the corner from the registration office in Dungannon, Co. Tyrone, where a large number of reporters were gathered. Jim Gibney and another republican went to see what was happening. They had had a phone call only minutes earlier from Noel Maguire, the only nationalist candidate (other than Bobby Sands) who had entered nomination papers for a by-election in Fermanagh/South Tyrone, but he had yet to arrive at the office to withdraw his papers and the deadline was drawing near. Adams had no doubt that if Maguire did not arrive in time, he was going to walk into the registration office and withdraw Sands' papers. That was what had been agreed. He had a statement in his pocket announcing Sands' withdrawal. Then Maguire's car drew up. He walked silently past the waiting reporters and into the registration office, to come out moments later with his nomination papers in his hand.

'It has become a question of conscience with me,' he said. 'I have been told the only way of saving Bobby Sands' life is by letting him go forward in the elections. I just cannot have the life of another man on my hands. I am calling on my supporters to throw their weight behind Bobby Sands.' Adams and Carron walked over and shook his hand.

The SDLP's Austin Currie had broken ranks with his party and declared that if Maguire withdrew his nomination, then he was going to enter his. An associate of Currie's was posted in Maguire's bar, where Noel Maguire had been waiting, ready to tip off Currie if there was any change of heart on Maguire's part. A game of bluff had been going on all day, with Currie watching Maguire who was watching Sinn Féin. But when Currie's associate went to call him to tell him of Maguire's intention to withdraw, he could not get access to a telephone line. All the lines were kept busy until the deadline for entering nominations had passed and Sands was left with a clear field.

Adams tore up the withdrawal statement. Provisional Sinn Féin were to take part in a general election in Northern Ireland.

By the closing day for nominations Bobby Sands had been thirty-two days in hospital and had lost 11.3 kilos. Inside the H-Blocks, he heard the news that he was now the only nationalist candidate in the Fermanagh/South Tyrone by-election. He wrote a note to Adams, signed with his penname 'Marcella', and had it smuggled out.[5]

To Brownie from Marcella, 2.4.81.

Well comrade Mór, how are ya! Got your note. Seems we've well and truly entered new realms. Hopefully we'll be successful if only for the Movement's sake. I'm getting the days in, they fly in. Feel myself getting naturally and gradually weaker. I will be very sick in a week or two, but my mind will see me thru. I've no doubt about that. Seen ya on TV, ya big ugly hunk, you haven't changed a bit. I'm not at all building hopes on anything. I'm afraid I'm just resigned to the worst, so sin sin. People find this hard to grasp altho' I'm ensuring I give my family some hope to hold onto. I've been reading poetry and Gaeilge in the papers and listening to whatever traditional music there is on the radio and generally carrying on – so for a change I'm taking it easy (such an excuse, are ye jealous?). Watch your big self and Beannacht Dé ort comrade.
Marcella

After he had seen Sands win a clear field in the election, Adams spent some time touring the constituency to test the mood there. When he left for Belfast he was convinced that Sands would win. Meanwhile, there was the running of the hunger-strike. A committee of Sinn Féin and IRA people had been set up, with Adams heading it, to oversee the running of the protest. It had to be decided what was to be done once the prisoners began to die, if they were to die. While some argued that the strike should be called off once the first four had died if nothing had been achieved, it was decided that the best thing would be for each hunger-striker who died to be replaced by another.

The schoolteacher, Owen Carron, had been appointed election agent for Sands and as Sands could not communicate with the media, Carron became the centre of the media coverage. Republicans poured into the constituency to work on the campaign. (Adams took charge of the Dungannon office.) Sinn Féin workers were getting their first taste of electioneering, and were having to learn on their feet. There was only a couple of weeks between the closing of the nominations and polling day. The only opponent was a local farmer, the Official Unionist, Harry West, who had held the seat before it had been taken from him by the independent nationalist, Frank Maguire. While the constituency had a majority of nationalists, many of them did not vote for Sands since they felt this would constitute a vote for the IRA campaign of violence and death. The area had a tradition for high turn-outs and as election day approached the pace of electioneering reached a frenzy.

On polling day itself, 8 April 1981, the Labour Party spokesman on Northern Ireland made an appeal from the House of Commons to people not to vote for Sands. 'A vote for Sands is a vote of approval for the perpetrators of the La Mon massacre, the murder of Lord Mountbatten, and the latest brutal and inhuman killing of Mrs Mathers.' (A census which was underway in Northern Ireland was being opposed by the republicans, as a gesture in solidarity with the hunger-strikers. In Derry some days before the election, a young woman, Joanna Mathers, had been making some extra money for her young family by collecting census forms. A masked man ran up to her, grabbed the census forms from her hand, put a gun to her head, and shot her dead.)

At the end of the day the ballot boxes were flown in army helicopters to Enniskillen, where the count was to take place the next day, 9 April. Adams, who had spent the day touring all the booths in the constituency and meeting strong animosity from the loyalists he met, spent the night in Enniskillen and the next day drove off alone across the border on his way to report to Ó Brádaigh. As the election result was read out, the red Ford Escort he was driving along the Slane road to Dublin began to swerve between the hedgerows on both sides as he started to pound the steering wheel and shout: 'Fuck it, we've done it, we've done it, we've done it…'[6]

Sands, Bobby, Anti-H-Block-Armagh, Political Prisoner, had won over 30,000 votes, 1,446 more than Harry West. He was now the 'Honourable Member for Fermanagh/South Tyrone'. A convicted member of the organisation which the British government had sought to criminalise had been elected to the House of Commons.

Dáil Elections

Sands' nomination, the election campaign and his overwhelming success – all against the background of his slow and painful demise – made headlines the world over and dealt a shattering blow to all the British government's efforts to put forward a picture of constitutional normality in Northern Ireland. Once again the problem of the six counties had become an issue of international debate.

Nine days after his election, Bobby Sands, MP, was given the last rites by a Catholic priest. Two days later he was visited by three members of the Dáil, Síle de Valera, Neil Blaney and Dr John O'Connell. Sands outlined the reasons for the protest and refused a request to end his fast. O'Connell, a medical doctor, estimated the prisoner would only survive for a few more days. Tension in the six counties was mounting steadily as Sands' death approached. Loyalist paramilitaries were talking about preparing for a civil war. The British government remained intransigent and the people of Northern Ireland waited in fear of the consequences of the inevitable death. On 29 April Adams received a letter from Brendan MacFarlane, who had replaced Sands as OC inside Long Kesh (Maze).[7] MacFarlane (Bik) was a former seminarian who had left to join the IRA and who was serving a sentence for the bombing of the Protestant Bayodo Bar in Belfast in August 1976, which resulted in the deaths of five people.

Comrade Mór, got your very welcome comm today. Good to hear from you. This is really some situation, isn't it? A terrific thought struck me two days ago and that was that there was every possibility the Brits will not say anything at all or make any attempt at dipping in attractive offers, but just stand back and let things run their course. I think your analysis of the Brit mentality is about as close as anyone can come, ie their stupidity is unbelievable. I still don't think they have learned that oppression breeds resistance and further oppression – further resistance! As for their arrogance – I never saw the likes of it (of course I'm not a much travelled individual but I reckon I'd have to go a long way to meet persons of a similar 'superior' nature). However, as you said, they will regret their stupidity. How I wish I were out – just to light the blue touch paper and retire if you know what I mean! Old habits die hard though some of mine had to be redirected as you well know. Anyway, one day I'll make a few noises in the right sectors....

As you know I saw Bob [Bobby Sands] on Saturday – it was quite an experience and in all honesty I haven't felt the same since. I just had a short yarn with him and when I was preparing to leave he said quietly: 'I'm dying Bik.' Don't think I can describe how I felt just then. I couldn't say anything except God Bless. I told him I'd see him again very soon and he just gave a quiet laugh. Man, what a feeling!!....

On Tuesday, 5 May 1981, at 1.17am Bobby Sands, who had lapsed into a coma, died in the presence of his parents, his brother Seán and sister Marcella. Thirty-five minutes later the Northern Ireland Office issued a short statement: 'He took his own life by refusing food and medical intervention for 66 days'. Widespread rioting broke out in Belfast, Derry and Dublin. MarFarlane wrote to Adams from his prison cell.[8] 'Comrade Mór, I have just heard the news – I'm shattered – just can't believe it. This is a terrible feeling I have. I don't even know what to say. Comrade, I'm sorry, but I just can't say anything else. May God in his infinite mercy grant eternal rest to his soul. Jesus Christ protect and guide us all. God Bless. Bik.' He also wrote to the three remaining hunger-strikers – Francis Hughes, Raymond McCreesh and Patsy O'Hara – who were now in hospital

Sands' body was taken to his family home in the Twinbrook Estate in West Belfast where it lay in state in an open coffin as friends, family and IRA comrades filed past. The funeral took place the following Thursday and a crowd of 100,000 people lined the route from the local church, St Luke's, to the republican plot at Milltown. Adams presided over the funeral and the oration was read out by Owen Carron. Inside the H-Blocks, the prisoners stood to attention behind the steel doors of their cells as one of them read out an oration in honour of their dead comrade.

Within two weeks, Sands' three hunger-striking companions were dead. Hughes died on his fifty-ninth day of fasting, McCreesh and O'Hara both on their sixty-first day of fasting. Joe McDonnell took the place of Sands. As the next three died their places were taken by others. Meanwhile efforts to end the protest by priests from the Irish Commission for Justice and Peace, a Catholic Church body, continued frantically. But the British remained intransigent, denouncing the protesters as murderers who were bringing their misery onto themselves. Brendan McLoughlin, who had joined the protest on 14 May, developed a perforated ulcer and had to be taken off his fast. There was time for consideration of how the protest was proceeding. Adams got a communication from MacFarlane:[9]

Comrade Mór, just heard that Brendan ended his hunger strike. He must be wrecked. Anyway, back to your comm and escalation. I went ahead and informed M [Martin] Hurson to embark on hunger strike on Monday next, but I think maybe we should bring him forward to

Saturday as a replacement for Brendan...

The situation will now become somewhat relaxed while we wait until Joe approaches the crucial stages. We must hold the position now. These Free State elections will give us a good opener. We talked here also on the 'balance of power' aspect. If we are successful enough we could cause a formidable threat to [Charles] Haughey alright. I accept what you say about 'no magic formula' and I realise that hard work on the ground is the only answer. Perhaps I expect too much too soon, but it's just that I'm anxious to get a settlement here as quickly as possible, hence my push in all directions at one time – just getting the boot into anything that moves and isn't on our side. The revolutionary effect would not manifest itself quickly anyway regardless of the inability to exploit the situation. It would still take time to build and mould our people into what is necessary for a successful push forward. The Free State does present difficulties. There is just really no comparison between the people down there and those in the north. I think they need a rude awakening which I believe we are presently doing. Once the swing has started then we are on our way, remembering of course the 'hand-crank' at all times. We'll see how it goes down there shortly. Just thinking there (dangerous pastime indeed) – if Martin goes on Saturday, what about commencing escalation say next Friday with another man. I'll get back to you on this again, once I have the lists of vols [volunteers] sorted out. I really do sympathise with your problem of those wishing to kill dead things. They're at it in here. God bless. Bik.

On 21 May, another incident took place that was to raise the profile of the hunger-strikers. The twenty-first Dáil had been dissolved and a general election called for 11 June in the Republic. Nine H-Block candidates were put forward and Adams was hoping that they might win the balance of power in a 'hung Dáil' scenario. In the event they managed to have two men elected – Paddy Agnew, a blanket man who topped the poll in Co. Louth, and Kieran Doherty, a hunger-striker who was elected in the Cavan/Monaghan constituency. In all, the republican candidates won 40,000 votes. The results were unexpected and caused consternation in the Republic. It was as much as Adams could have hoped for. He received a letter from MacFarlane about the result.[10]

We have certainly caused a stir. Looks like Garret [Fitzgerald] would form a government depending of course on his relationship with Cluskey's boys [the Labour Party]. Regardless of who forms a government it will be extremely shaky. Well we have effected the political change you spoke of. Congratulations, oh wise one!...

He also wrote of a visit from the Northern Ireland priest Fr Denis

Faul and of how he had explained to him 'that our strategy was designed to maintain and increase pressure on the Brits and that we aimed for a settlement as quickly as possible with as little loss also'. He added that the impression seemed to be gaining ground outside the prison that the prisoners were having their decisions made for them by the IRA. This would be a dangerous development, he wrote, and it should be rectified.

The Haughey government was replaced by a coalition of Fine Gael and Labour, with Garret Fitzgerald as Taoiseach. None of the Republic's parties gave support to the call for the five demands. In the British parliament, a new piece of legislation was being prepared, the Representation of the People Act, which would prohibit prisoners from standing for parliament. At the beginning of June, MacFarlane got permission from the outside leadership for a small escalation in the protest, and a fifth prisoner, Tom McElwee, went on hunger-strike. The Irish Commission for Justice and Peace negotiators were desperately trying to find a way around the impasse which had developed in their talks with the authorities. Unknown to them however the British were having secret negotiations with the IRA. Adams feared that the Commission might get the hunger-strikers to come off their fast for less than what the Foreign Office had already promised in the secret talks, so he telephoned the Commission and arranged to meet two of those involved, Fr Oliver Crilly and Hugh Logue, in a safe house in Belfast. The two men were astonished when they were told that the British were offering the IRA more than they were offering the Commission. They were being used as an intelligence feed, Adams told the men. Following this talk, the Commission sought confirmation of the secret negotiations from the Northern Ireland Office (NIO) in Belfast. The Foreign Office were annoyed at the breaking of confidence, but the negotiations continued.

Adams was in constant contact with MacFarlane, who was keeping him up to date with developments inside the H-Blocks and discussing strategy with him. MacFarlane feared that the SDLP, the Catholic Church and the Dublin government were undermining the support that existed among nationalists for the hunger-strikers. The Commission's proposals were causing them great difficulties. MacFarlane wrote the following to Adams on 28 June:[11]

> Families of hunger-strikers appear ready to grab what comes as a
> feasible settlement. It will, I believe, be attractive enough to satisfy the
> Church, etc, of Brit flexibility and in time they will look to us for a
> response, ie, terminate the hunger strike.... If we choose to continue with

the strike we will be faced with a situation whereby Joe will die, followed by others and after x amount of deaths public opinion will hammer us into the ground, forcing us to end the hunger strike... a shattering defeat into the bargain.... If we can combat the undermining successfully and eliminate the prospect of crushing defeat after further deaths then I feel we should at least maintain our position. I know this could well mean Joe's death and possibly others before we reach a settlement, but if a settlement is obtainable we should try for it.

Two days later in another letter MacFarlane is again agonising over what should be done:[12]

If it doesn't appear that the Brits will be forthcoming with a feasible settlement, then we should get in before public opinion swings against us, forcing us to halt after say six or seven deaths, which would be a disaster. I do not want the war to suffer any setbacks, like public condemnation of the movement. We have made major gains to date, which is what we are all about.

Meanwhile, as the death of Joe McDonnell grew closer and closer, the Commission had received an assurance from the NIO that an official would be sent into Long Kesh to confirm a deal they had been discussing. But the official never came, despite the repeated promises from the NIO. In the early hours of 5 July, 30-year-old Joe McDonnell died after 61 days on hunger-strike. Adams had spent the night waiting for a telephone call from his Foreign Office contact. He never called. MacFarlane wrote to Adams from inside his cell:

Comrade, just got confirmation that Joe died this morning. God rest his soul.

The moment the news was released, rioting broke out in Belfast. A 33-year-old woman, Nora McCabe, died when she was hit by a plastic bullet shot from a passing police Land-rover as she walked to the local shop. Further down the Falls Road, at just after 5am, John Dempsey, a 16-year-old member of Na Fianna, was shot dead when he and a number of other youths crashed through the gates of a bus depot in a stolen van and began to hurl petrol and acid bombs at the two soldiers on guard. Later that day MacFarlane wrote to Adams:[13]

Comrade Mór, got your comm today alright. I was wrecked when I read it. The whole thing could have been settled by now. You must be worn out, cara. I know what happened surprised the Brits [McDonnell's death]. I sat here this morning and cursed them from the high heavens.

I had a good idea they were operating every bloody angle they could land their hands on to outflank us some and take Joe to the brink. What a tragedy....

Adams wrote a piece which was published, under the pen-name Brownie, the following week in *An Phoblacht*.[14] Titled 'Tribute to a young republican', he wrote about the 16-year-old Dempsey boy who had been shot as he crashed in through the bus depot. For Adams his death was 'a stark reminder that for the first time in contemporary Irish history, the struggle has crossed the generation gap'.

He attended Dempsey's funeral and arrived late for McDonnell's, which was on the same day. As the mourners filed down Shaw Street in West Belfast, he grew uneasy with the way the security forces were acting. Outside the Busy Bee shopping centre, the procession stopped for a gun salute. (Sands' tribute had taken place at the same spot.) Three men with black berets and uniforms came out of the crowd, raised rifles to their shoulders and fired a volley of shots. Then they slipped back into the crowd and began to make their way to the pre-arranged safe house.

Adams tried to intervene, but it was too late. The procession moved forward, on its way up to the republican plot where McDonnell was to be buried beside Bobby Sands. Up in the air the path of the three gunmen was being monitored by a soldier in an army helicopter, who was radioing their movements to troops below. He saw the men enter a house and gave the address to the troops, who immediately rushed to seal it off. One ran around to the back of the house and saw a man about to climb out a kitchen window, with a rifle in his hand. 'Army, stop or I'll fire', he shouted, but the man made to climb back into the house. The soldier fired one shot and the man fell into the kitchen. When the back door of the house was kicked in, Paddy Adams, younger brother of Gerry, was found lying on the floor clutching his side, and a rifle was lying on the window-sill. He was later sentenced to four and a half years.

Three days passed and the sixth hunger-striker – Martin Hurson (26) – died on the forty-sixth day of his fast. MacFarlane wrote to Adams:[15]

Comrade Mór, we heard around 11am about Martin's tragic death. In all honesty, it has been the biggest shock to date and has left me shattered. No way was anyone even thinking of Martin as anywhere near the danger mark. I can only assume that the infection in his stomach has somehow been the cause of his untimely death. May God have mercy on his soul. I will have to move immediately with his replacement. It will be Matt Devlin (Tyrone). He was on the second squad of the first hunger-strike. This means that the usual clearance procedure will be skipped over. You'll have to accept my judgement on his being sound. He is fully aware of exactly what his hunger-strike means – i.e. that in a short period he stands to lose his life.

In further secret negotiations the IRA were not happy with what the British were offering, but the British insisted that it was as far as they could go. The IRA leadership, in turn, said that they could not undermine their comrades in the prison by accepting such terms and that the prisoners would reject them anyway. They were as surprised as anyone by the lengths to which the prisoners were prepared to go to get their demands. They had tried to prevent the hunger-strike and wanted it ended. Any political advantage won from it had not been planned, they said. There was deadlock in the negotiations.

Adams wrote to MacFarlane, outlining the position reached in the secret talks.[16] MacFarlane replied:

I fully agree with the two options you outlined. It is either a settlement or it isn't. No room for half measures and meaningless cosmetic exercises. Better to be straight about it and just come out and say sin é – no more! Now to maintain position and forge ahead, it looks like a costly venture indeed. However, after careful consideration of the overall situation I believe it would be wrong to capitulate. We took a decision and committed ourselves to hunger-strike action.... I feel the part we played in forwarding the liberation struggle has been great. Terrific gains have been made and the Brits are losing by the day.

On 27 July MacFarlane again wrote to Adams and brought up the issue of contesting elections in the Irish Republic:

We've been thinking of various ways to exploit our situation to the full for maximum gain on the ground, especially in the Free State. The climate now is ripe to make significant progress and establish a firm base down there which is a necessity for future development and success in the final analysis.... We are examining the possibility of contesting elections and actually making full use of seats gained – ie participating in the Dáil. Such an idea presents problems within the movement. How great would the opposition be and what would be the consequences of pursuing a course which did not enjoy a sizeable degree of support?... Anyway we are thinking along these lines at present. It isn't a universal line of thought as yet. In fact it's pretty much restricted to a few.[17]

On Tuesday, 28 July, following the death of Martin Hurson, Dungannon headmaster Fr Denis Faul decided it was time to get the relatives to bring the hunger-strike to an end. He telephoned them and arranged for a meeting in Toomebridge that night. When they assembled he told them that the strike had reached an impasse and that it was time to call it off. The IRA were an army and they could order the men to end their fast. Brendan MacFarlane had told him that 'the buck stops with Gerry Adams', he told the relatives. After some debate it was decided that Adams should be confronted and the issue thrashed out with him. The Sinn Féin HQ was telephoned and while Adams could not come to Toomebridge for security reasons (the telephone was undoubtedly bugged), if the relatives came to Belfast he would see them there.

The relatives crowded into cars and drove straight to Belfast. An argument lasting a number of hours began, with Adams holding his own against the relatives and Fr Faul. Adams insisted that the Army Council could not order the men to end their fast and had, in fact, been against the strike in the first place. He rejected a suggestion from Fr Faul that he go to the prison and persuade the men to come off their fast. He began to say that it would be difficult for him to get in contact with people on the Army Council and that it would take some time. Fr Faul did not believe this and began to flatter Adams about his debating skills, praising him for the way he had managed, for hours on end, to single-handedly argue with both him and the relatives. But the flattery did not work, and Faul and the relatives left without having had any of their demands satisfied.

However, the next morning Adams telephoned the priest and said he was ready to go to the prison and explain exactly what the position was to the hunger-strikers. Permission for Adams, Owen Carron and an Irish Republican Socialist Party man, Seamus Reddy, to enter the prison was quickly arranged.

Fr Faul's success at getting Adams to visit the prisoners was, in his mind, tempered by the presence of Carron. Carron was the candidate in the by-election caused by Sands' death, and the priest felt that the schoolteacher's presence on the prison visit would, by itself, make the prisoners less likely to come off their fast. He believed they would feel obliged to wait at least until after voting day.

Adams and his two companions met with MacFarlane and six of the hunger-strikers in the hospital canteen – Tom McElwee, Paddy Quinn, Laurence McKeown, Pat McGeown, Matt Devlin and Mickey Devine. Kieran Doherty and Kevin Lynch, both of whom were seriously weakened by their fast, remained in their beds in the nearby wards. Adams was apprehensive about meeting the men, with their unhealthy looking skin stretched on their almost fleshless skulls and their big glazed eyes. McElwee offered him some of their mineral water, in Irish, and when Adams took a large gulp, joked that the water was expensive and that Adams should go easy on it.

Adams outlined to them what the British were willing to concede if they ended their fast now. He said he did not believe that the British were willing to concede anything else in the short term. He told them that if they, collectively or individually, decided to come off the hunger-strike, then that decision would be respected and welcomed. 'You eight could be dead and another five or six could be dead and you still might not get your five demands,' he said. As Carron and Reddy addressed the starving men, Adams stole a look at their emaciated condition. He had drunk two jugs of water and McElwee joked as he went to refill the jug that they wouldn't have him in again.

Adams then went to see Doherty and told him he would be dead in a week and that he could announce it was over now. 'Thatcher can't break us, I'm no criminal,' replied Doherty. Lynch was in too bad a condition to be seen, but Adams met his father who was greatly upset and shouted at Adams, 'You're responsible. My son is dying in there… why don't you take them off it?' Adams replied that he could not take them off the strike, but that he, the father, could.

When Paddy Quinn's condition deteriorated and he began having fits, his family were called. His mother was not allowed to see him, since it was felt it would cause her too much distress. Another family member went into his room and emerged looking ill, saying that Paddy was dying. The man was screaming in agony and down the corridor the mothers of Kevin Lynch and Kieran Doherty were trying to block out the noise. Mrs Quinn was taken to see the prison doctor. She asked what her son's chances were if he was taken off the fast. Fifty-fifty, she was told. 'I'm taking him off,' she declared.

On 1 August the seventh hunger-striker to die, Kevin Lynch (25), passed away peacefully on the seventy-first day of his fast. MacFarlane wrote to Adams:

> The pressure appears to be hardening in the direction of the A/C [Army Council] to call a halt. Do you want a statement from us outlining the position in regard to hunger-strike? I've just told Ricky to get down a paragraph or two on A/C moral obligation aspect and, if you feel it helps, bang it out. Don't mean to jump the gun by us stating A/C policy. Just felt a need to say something....[18]

The next day, Kieran Doherty died on his seventy-third day without food. He had been elected TD for Cavan/Monaghan in the June elections in the Republic. The next day, Monday, the flags on Government Buildings in Dublin were flown at half-mast.

On Thursday, the RUC released figures on violence since the beginning of the hunger-strike: fifty-one had died, ten of them policemen and thirteen of them soldiers. Over 1,000 had been injured and 1,700 had been arrested.

On Saturday, the ninth hunger striker to die, Thomas McElwee (23), passed away on the sixty-second day of his fast. Two people died in the riots in Belfast that night.

Ballot Box and Armalite

The by-election to fill the Fermanagh/South Tyrone seat vacated by the death of Bobby Sands was called for 20 August. Due to the new British legislation, the republicans could no longer nominate a prisoner. Following a lengthy debate, it was decided to put Owen Carron forward as the candidate, although some thought this was crossing the line to Sinn Féin itself getting involved in British government elections. The SDLP decided to accept the decision of its constituency branch, which had voted by a narrow margin not to contest the election. The unionists selected a unity candidate, a major in the UDR, Ken Magennis. The Alliance Party and Sinn Féin the Workers' Party (which had grown out of Official Sinn Féin) also entered the contest. Carron was elected with a greater majority than Sands.

On the day of Carron's electoral success the tenth hunger-striker passed away. Mickey Devine (27) died on the sixtieth day of his fast. In a nearby bed, hunger-striker Pat McGeown was falling in and out of consciousness. He felt the priest give him the last rites, then he drifted off again. His family decided to have him taken off the fast and after the necessary papers were signed, the unconscious man was given medication.

Ten days later, on 31 August, MacFarlane wrote to Adams on the problem of families intervening when the hunger-strikers lost consciousness:

> I think we have done everything in our power to combat this, so we can only wait and see. It wrecks me to think that the breaking power lies with those who haven't a clue what our struggle is all about. I'm serious – I'm shattered even thinking about it. I only pray we can overcome it. The boys are 100% sound as you know.... [19]

On 4 September Matt Devlin was taken off his fast by his relatives. Two days later the same occurred with Laurence McKeown, who had been seventy days on hunger-strike, four days longer than Bobby Sands. Carron asked Thatcher and Fitzgerald if he could meet them; Fitzgerald refused, but Thatcher said he could meet the Secretary of State's deputy, Michael Allison, which he did but to no avail.

On Sunday, 27 September, Fr Faul called a meeting for the relatives of the hunger-strikers, at which a number of them pledged that when their sons or husbands fell unconscious, they would give instructions that he be given medical attention and saved. It was another body blow to the tottering protest. A new Secretary of State, James Prior, had been appointed and was busying himself trying to end the hunger-strike. He had arrived at the right time to do so. On Saturday afternoon, 3 October 1981, after 217 days, the hunger-strike was officially called off by the prisoners. MacFarlane wrote a 'comm' to Adams, detailing all that had happened inside the H-Blocks and how the prisoners felt. He ended his letter, 'Regards to all the boyos. Take care and God bless. PS: I'm tired man! Bik'.

At the 1980 Ard Fheis, Sinn Féin members had voted against running in the local elections in May in Northern Ireland. The leadership had been trying to inch the party towards a 'positive attitude to elections' but was meeting with resistance to the idea. The suspicion that 'politics' was something incompatible with the war effort and inevitably led to a betrayal of republicanism was deeply rooted in the movement. However, at the 1981 Ard Fheis in November of that year the scene had changed entirely. A motion was passed that Sinn Féin 'adopt a positive approach to future electoral contests'. It was decided that the party would now contest local elections in the North as it had been doing in the Republic. Seats won would be taken. It was also decided to give the Ard Comhairle the authority to decide on whether or not to contest Westminster, Leinster House or Stormont elections on an abstentionist basis. Adams, in an address to the delegates, said the hunger-strike had led 'to a mini-revival of nationalist consciousness, especially amongst young people', and that the H-Block prisoners had brought the national question back into the centre of the political stage. Republicans would now have to mobilise on all issues in the future, otherwise the prisoners would have died in vain.

Danny Morrison, in his address, delivered lines which came to sum up the new Provisional strategy in the popular mind. 'Who

here really believes that we can win the war through the ballot box?'
he asked. Then, after a pause, he went on. 'But will anyone here
object if with a ballot paper in this hand and an Armalite in this
hand, we take power in Ireland?'

Just how much work lay ahead of the party if they wished to use
this dual strategy to 'take power in Ireland' was aptly illustrated the
following February, when Sinn Féin contested the general election
in the Republic – not on an emotional issue but as a political party
in contest with the other political parties in the twenty-six counties.
Their vote was a huge drop on that won during the hunger-strike
and showed the large gap that lay between electoral intervention
and electoral strategy – a gap which Adams was all too aware of. In
the South, he warned, a long hard task of building a real and
relevant political party – almost out of nothing – had to begin.

9: Gerry Adams, MP

In February 1982 Sinn Féin announced that it was going to contest the Assembly elections in Northern Ireland. The elections were to select members for a new forum, which James Prior hoped would lead to an end to the political deadlock which existed in the six counties. Assembly members would be elected by proportional representation and while initially the new forum would have few if any powers, power would be handed over to it in a piecemeal fashion if cross-community support could be demonstrated. The idea was termed 'rolling devolution'.

Initially, Sinn Féin was in favour of boycotting the elections, but as the SDLP had decided to enter them, the party opted to take part. There were strong reservations among many in Northern Ireland, Dublin and London, about proceeding with the project at all. Many thought it was doomed to failure and could only worsen the situation in the six counties. The IRA was noticeably inactive during the run-up to polling day. There were reports of discontent and disputes in the IRA ranks because of this first ever all-out electoral adventure by Sinn Féin which, it was feared, would lead to a long-term de-escalation of the war effort.

Assembly Candidate

Adams began an intensive campaign in his West Belfast constituency, touring the area with a dozen or so election workers and promising to have all sorts of minor problems, like broken pavements and streetlights, taken up and pursued by Sinn Féin activists with the city's local authorities. There was also a massive registration campaign, as the republicans urged people who normally took no part in elections to register and vote for Sinn Féin.

The elections took place on 20 October and changed the face of northern Irish politics forever. Adams, Morrison, McGuinness, Carron and Jim McAllister were elected on the Sinn Féin ticket. Sinn Féin won 64,191 first-preference votes, 10.2 per cent of the total cast and 35 per cent of the total number of nationalist votes. The SDLP won 118,891 votes, being 18.8 per cent of the first preference total, and giving them fourteen seats. Analysts said that the republican vote had partly come from moderate nationalists, but mostly from the mobilisation of new voters.

'It is a serious matter that so many in the community believe the gun is the only solution to political problems,' said the SDLP leader John Hume after the results of the poll became known. 'Mr Prior's Assembly is as dead as a dodo.'[1]

Prior, however, announced that the Assembly would go ahead as planned, but would not say if he intended inviting Sinn Féin representatives to any discussions between the parties needed to set it up. The Revd Ian Paisley said he would accept a Sinn Féin presence in the Assembly if its abstentionist policy was dropped, but he would talk to its representatives only in the chamber and not in private. He accepted that the Sinn Féin vote had been the expression of a democratic opinion.

The newspapers reported the poll as giving a credibility and legitimacy to the IRA which would shock many and that the criminalisation policy, based on the assumption that a small insignificant minority provided the base for the IRA, was wrong. The result was also evidence of the increasing polarisation which was occurring in the six counties, the papers said. Prior was condemned for giving the republicans such an opportunity to show the extent of their support. They had stood in seven of the twelve constituencies. Adams had topped the poll in West Belfast as had Carron in Fermanagh/South Tyrone, McAllister was elected in Armagh, McGuinness in Derry and Morrison in Mid-Ulster.

Adams was the first candidate elected in the six counties. He won 9,700 votes in his West Belfast constituency, more than the combined votes of the SDLP candidates he was competing with. In Belfast's City Hall he delivered a short acceptance speech as the security forces and unionist supporters looked on. He announced his intention to contest the West Belfast seat at the next general election and challenged the sitting MP, Gerry Fitt, to resign his seat now and fight a by-election. He was sure, he said, that the IRA was happy with Sinn Féin's performance in the elections. His photograph as he left the hall surrounded by supporters was printed on the front page of many Irish and British newspapers the next day.

The SDLP's win of fourteen seats put them five down on the 1973 Assembly elections. Adams saw the Sinn Féin vote as a significant step towards it's objective of becoming the majority nationalist party. It was later reported that Sinn Féin had topped the poll on expenditure during the elections. The party had spent more than £27,000 on their campaign, with Danny Morrison spending £3,925. Martin McGuinness had spent £3,629, and Adams had spent £1,971. The SDLP's John Hume spent £1,390, and unionists Jim Molyneaux and the Revd Ian Paisley spent £749 and £1,210 respectively.

The week after the Assembly elections Sinn Féin held its 1982 Ard Fheis in Dublin and voted by the required two-thirds majority to get rid of the policy of federalism from the party's constitution. The federalism policy envisaged a united Ireland divided into the four ancient provinces, with the old nine-county Ulster forming one of the federal divisions. The young northerners disliked this policy; they believed that such a unit would leave the loyalists with too significant a proportion of the power. The dropping of the policy was a personal blow to Ó Brádaigh who had fought for its retention during Ard Comhairle debates. He felt his position was being undermined, but he was persuaded to remain on as President for another year. The changes in the party leadership and the direction of party policy were also the result of a North-South divide developing in the movement.

Sinn Féin now began to prepare for the forthcoming British general election. Four advice centres had been opened in West Belfast in October 1982 and the intensive registration campaign continued. Disquiet about this immersion into political activity also continued among party members. This was partly because republicans who had seen themselves as being involved in revolutionary warfare now discovered they were in a movement which was dealing with all the minor difficulties and complaints addressed to a political party when trying to build political support. Also, vast sums of money were now being put into attracting voters rather than paying for the war. In addition, electoralism had a direct influence on the war by prohibiting actions which could be considered assaults on the party constituency. Armed robberies in such places as West Belfast were gradually ended and it was attempted to change from the policy of 'knee-capping' anti-social elements to something more constructive.

However, as long as the new venture into electoralism continued to ride on the crest of a wave, the critics were in effect silenced. Following Sinn Féin's successes in the 1982 Assembly elections the party began to forge links with the left of the Labour Party in Britain. Adams and Morrison were invited to London to County Hall for talks with Labour Party members of the Greater London Council. The visit was to take place on 14 December, but the violence in Northern Ireland was to intervene. In Ballykelly, near Derry city, a bomb was planted by the INLA in the Droppin' Well pub, a crowded disco lounge where British soldiers from the nearby barracks met with local girls. Sixteen people were killed and sixty-six injured. Two days later, the man who ten years earlier had met with Adams in a luxurious house on the banks of the Thames, British Home Secretary, William Whitelaw, issued Adams and Morrison with exclusion orders, banning them from Britain under the Prevention of Terrorism Act. (The act allows the government to do so for anyone 'involved in the commission, preparation, or instigation of acts of terrorism'.) Then in January, the RUC refused gun permits to Adams and McGuinness, although they are normally granted to elected representatives in Northern Ireland. The decision was announced soon after a court heard a UVF man say Adams was on their hit list. The UDA magazine, *Ulster*, that month carried a wanted, dead or alive, poster of Adams.

Gerry Adams, MP

At the beginning of May 1983 Adams candidature for the Westminster elections was officially announced. McGuinness went forward in Derry. Sinn Féin went into top gear and put in action all that it had learned about elections since the Sands victory only two years previously. Dozens of new advice centres were opened and by the end of the election Adams could boast that there were thirty-eight such centres in his constituency.[2]

In the first week in June John Hume launched an attack on the Provisionals. He claimed that while Sinn Féin campaigned for better jobs and houses, the IRA were blowing up workplaces and houses and discouraging foreign investment in Northern Ireland. The Provisionals were creating and exploiting unemployment, he said. 'What we are saying to the people of Northern Ireland is that you have a clear choice – build or destroy.'[3]

If what Hume said was correct, then a significant proportion of the population of the six counties opted for destruction. The republicans were elated with the result of the election, which saw them increasing their percentage of the vote in the six counties from 10.1 per cent to 13.4 per cent of the total, an increase of 3.3 per cent. They were making steady progress in their attempt to overtake the SDLP as the majority voice of northern nationalists. The moderate nationalists had won 17.9 per cent of the vote, down nearly 1 per cent on the Assembly elections. They won only one seat, in Derry, where Hume topped the poll. In the Mid-Ulster constituency Danny Morrison came within seventy-eight votes of winning a seat. Again, Sinn Féin had managed to bring out new voters.

The Dublin government expressed concern at this rising vote for a party which supported violence when the SDLP were offering a constitutional alternative, and said the result made even more urgent the search for a peaceful political solution. On the following Sunday, however, the Irish Foreign Affairs Minister, Peter Barry, said the vote was not a vote for violence but rather a warning from the Catholic community that it would no longer tolerate the lack of political movement. It was, he said, 'ludicrous' to see Sinn Féin campaigning for better housing; a recent IRA bomb had destroyed 200 homes. 'And now these people say they are concerned about housing conditions,' the Minister said.

Adams had topped the poll in his constituency, becoming the 'Honourable Member for West Belfast'. He won a majority of more than 5,000 votes over his nearest rival, Dr Joe Hendron of the SDLP, winning in all 16,379 votes. In a somewhat subdued acceptance speech in the crowded City Hall, with the police and his political opponents looking on, Adams described his victory as 'an historic event' which would 'permanently alter electoral politics in Northern Ireland'. He called on the British government to use their return to power as an opportunity to bring about peace in Ireland. 'The British government, now a strong British government, have the opportunity to bring about peace in this country. This morning a British soldier was killed in Ballymurphy. The responsibility for his death lies with the British government. The tragedy of Ireland rests with the British government. That British soldier should not have been in Northern Ireland.' He continued that he would represent all his constituents, regardless of their political or religious affiliations.

Adams' rival, the defeated MP, Gerry Fitt, said the vote was an unambiguous one for murder and bombing. However, Fitt was heartened by the fact that he had received votes from both Catholics and Protestants. (He had appealed to Protestants to vote for him in order to keep Adams out.) As Adams and his supporters left the Hall to make their way back to West Belfast in a triumphant motorcade, the unionist supporters shouted after them 'Murderers! Murderers!'.

Following Adams' election, the Labour Party's Ken Livingstone re-issued the invitation to visit London and the authorities withdrew the exclusion order. Adams arrived on 26 July to be greeted by the Labour MP Jeremy Crobyn and enormous media interest. Adams said his visit was aimed at 'breaking down the wall of disinformation' created by the British media so that he could address the British public directly. The major public meeting took place on a Wednesday night in Finsbury Town Hall. Adams and Joe

Austin shared a platform with the two Islington MPs, Jeremy
Corbyn and Chris Smith – who expressed his personal opposition
to the use of force to achieve British withdrawal and a united
Ireland, an outcome he supported – and Ken Livingstone and
Sheila Healy, the Labour Committee on Ireland representative.

In his speech, Adams said socialists in Britain must oppose the
'colonial stranglehold which the British government maintains
over our country'. There was, he said, 'complete harmony between
the fight for Irish freedom and the struggle of the working class in
Britain and Ireland for the overthrow of capitalism'.

Later that year, at a fringe meeting at the Labour Conference, he
called on Labour to re-examine its attitude and to work for Irish
unity, and accused the leadership of having played 'a disgraceful
role' in Ireland. He repeated his Finsbury message: 'There will
never be socialism in Ireland or in Britain, while Britain enslaves
Ireland'.

Three months later, on 16 December, an IRA team parked two
cars packed with explosives outside the Harrods department store
in London. A warning was telephoned and as the frightened
Christmas shoppers tried to flee the thronged shops and streets, the
blast cut through them, killing eight. Adams expressed regret, but
qualified it by saying he did not want to get involved in the 'politics
of condemnation'.

Supergrass Target

The IRA, like other paramilitary groups in Northern Ireland, were
suffering from a phenomenon which had been dubbed the 'supergrass', where uncorroborated evidence given by alleged members
of illegal groups would be used in 'Diplock' courts to jail large
numbers of people. The 'supergrass' would be given immunity and
a new name and life in another country. Most of the charges were
later thrown out by courts of appeal, but the people affected had
usually spent years in jail by that stage.

In September 1983 the RUC arrested a Belfast man called Robert
Lean, whom an alleged IRA member, William Skelly, had said had
been involved in a rocket attack and a knee-capping. Some newspapers reported that Lean was the second-in-command of the
Belfast Brigade and that senior IRA members had fled in order to
avoid arrest and conviction on information that Lean had given the
police following his arrest. He was reported to have informed on
twenty-eight people. At a rally attended by hundreds of people in
the Beechmount area, Adams addressed the crowd and raised the

issue of reports that he, Morrison, McGuinness and others had been informed upon and had fled. 'Danny Morrison and I are quite available to be arrested whenever the RUC wants to arrest us,' he said. But the arrests were never made.

Later that month at a Sinn Féin press conference Lean, who claimed to have escaped from Palace Barracks the previous night, appeared and told the assembled reporters that he was publicly retracting the evidence he had given the RUC. He claimed he had never been an IRA member and that the RUC had threatened and bribed him. Skelly had also implicated Lean's wife – they had five children – and when the police had shown him photographs and statements about events that people were allegedly involved in, he had signed the statements.

'They wanted Adams badly,' he said and they had concocted a statement relating to a supposed meeting he had been at with Adams and a number of other men, where the ending of IRA punishment-shootings were discussed. But he had refused to sign the statement, since he felt he could not have faced Adams in Castlereagh if he had been brought in. 'I have a lot of respect for Gerry Adams, and also I didn't want to put unnecessary pressure on my family: he's a very popular man in Belfast.'[4]

When he left the press conference, Lean was again arrested by the RUC. In November, Skelly, in turn, retracted his evidence.

Sinn Féin President

November 1983 was a month of elation and celebration for Sinn Féin, whose members felt they were on the crest of a wave and making rapid progress towards their objective. In the 17 November issue of *An Phoblacht*, which followed the Ard Fheis and the election of Adams as the party President, the language was triumphant. 'It [Sinn Féin] has declared itself firmly for an extensive political push in the twenty-six counties and a determined advance on its gains already achieved in the North', read the front page, under the headlines 'Facing the Future' and 'New Leadership'.[5] Referring to the decision to contest the coming EEC elections on an attendance basis, the paper read, 'Sinn Féin is poised to make the final thrust against the SDLP in the North, replacing it as the majority nationalist party there'. In the inside pages, a report stated that 'Last weekend's Sinn Féin Ard Fheis with an harmonious change of leadership as well as a significant decision in electoral strategy, can be justly described as a milestone in the party's long and dramatic history'.

At the Ard Fheis, some members said that the decision to accept any seats won in the EEC elections, while not against the constitution of the party, was against the spirit of the constitution. Martin McGuinness replied that 'to fight the EEC elections on an abstentionist basis would be madness when it provides the best opportunity ever to beat the SDLP'. Difference of opinion about electoralism was also illustrated by the defeat of one motion reaffirming the ban on discussing the policy of abstentionism, and the passing of another, by 208 votes to ninety-eight, that 'no aspect of the constitution and rules be closed to discussion'. Ó Brádaigh in his speech outlined a number of reasons why he was not seeking re-election; among these was his objection to sitting in the European Assembly, while Daithí Ó Connaill said he did not believe the leadership represented the organisation as a whole.

Adams, in his first presidential address, told the delegates that he was reluctant to take up the post since the emphasis needed to be on the twenty-six counties and he would prefer if the party was headed by someone from the South. His election did not represent a 'northern takeover' of the party, as was being said in some newspapers, nor did it mean he was going to lead the party into Leinster House. 'My election means neither of those things,' he said.

He went on to cover briefly many areas he was to give prominence to over the coming years. In the South Sinn Féin had become isolated and had failed to build on the economic and social momentum that the party had begun in the '60s, leaving others, who had abandoned the central issue of partition, to make political capital out of that work. (Sinn Féin The Workers' Party, now simply The Workers' Party, had a number of elected representatives in Dáil Éireann.) While the results of the February 1982 general election had been half those of the H-Block election vote in 1981, they still showed an encouraging base which could be worked on.

Adams continued with his view of the Republic, saying the true spirit of nationalism or independence was not fostered there because that would lead to the primary demand for an end to partition. The separate Irish culture which existed was being allowed to wither, the national language was being ignored and Irish culture transposed by an imported, mid-Atlantic pseudo-culture. In the South, Sinn Féin faced a great task. There would have to be a shake-up of the party publicity machine in Dublin.

'It needs to be made clear that republicans are not interested in armed struggle in the twenty-six counties, aimed at the takeover of the state', he said. What was wanted was 'democratic institutions of government with direct and relative popular control and participation'. Sinn Féin wanted a 'planned economy controlled by its workers'. There would be absolute neutrality. There would be the conditions for the development of a living, useful independent Irish culture – he called on everyone in the hall to educate themselves and learn the Irish language. But violence would continue in the six counties in the north-east of the island: 'Armed struggle is a necessary and morally correct form of resistance in the six counties against a government whose presence is rejected by the vast majority of Irish people,' he said to cheers and applause.

Adams' presidential speech also included a call to the Protestant people of Ireland, whom he saw playing their part in a democratic united Ireland. Less than a month later, on the morning of Wednesday, 7 December, just after he got out of his car, Official Unionist Assemblyman Edgar Graham was shot dead by the IRA. 'Incitement Answered' read the headline in the following day's *An Phoblacht*. 'A salutary lesson for those who incite sectarian violence against the Catholic people.' Just over a week later, on 16 December, in a wood near Ballinamore, Co. Leitrim, a garda and an Irish soldier were shot dead as an IRA unit made an escape bid from the hide-out where they had been holding the kidnapped chief executive of the Quinnsworth supermarket chain, Don Tidey.

Assessing the Past

In February 1984 Adams addressed a meeting of some 300 Sinn Féin members in Dublin, outlining to them his view of the last fifteen years in Ireland and Sinn Féin's current strategy. After 1969 when the struggle had a wide popular base, people were 'simply absorbed into' the republican movement, they were not educated into it. The strong movement that existed then was the basis for the fast-moving situation where, within three years, Stormont collapsed – an event which could not have taken place five years before. 'But the enemy learned more quickly than we did how to cope with the ongoing situation.'

The British had launched a counter-insurgency campaign and republicans suffered circumstances and conditions which were 'absolutely and unimaginably repressive.... Four to five years after 1969, the movement's base was starting to become narrow'. In the period around 1973 Sinn Féin had been a strong protest organisation, but it could not maintain its hold on supporters for more than short emotive periods. 'A person who couldn't join the fight or was worn out after a period in prison, couldn't really do very much and became basically a spectator.' The duration of the 1975 truce was a mistake. The British introduced normalisation, criminalisation, and the 'primacy of the RUC. No one was terribly concerned about these things, because many at the time thought the British were going to leave. The period confused 99 per cent of the republican base, and is, in my view, the one period in the last fifteen years when republicans were almost beaten, almost shattered.... In the six counties, the disillusionment and confusion was at a maximum'.

'Towards the end of that period,' Adams continued, 'republican leaders sat down and conducted a number of major reviews of the whole situation, not only to establish what had happened, because that was fairly clear, but to analyse what to do about it.' The review took between three and four months, after which a number of basic decisions were taken: 'That we had to get back to and update our republicanism, and that we had to establish a basic ideological unity so that the mistakes which were made in 1969 wouldn't happen again. The simple definition of what we were after was this: unless we can agree on where we are going, we're never going to agree on how to get there'. It was also agreed that the republicans' base had to be broadened, that the community support which existed previously had to be won back, that the spectator politics had to cease and that a party had to be built which could develop on the basis of a thirty-two-county strategy:

> Around the time of Jimmy Drumm's speech at Bodenstown [in 1977], when we told republicans that the British were not getting out, there was a return of confidence amongst republicans that the struggle wasn't over. At the same time, as we have been told by IRA spokespersons in numerous interviews since, the IRA had also carried out a review and re-organisation, and were able to rebuild strength and confidence... . With ongoing discussions as to how these ideas could best be developed politically, someone suggested electoral interventions. There had been earlier discussion, back in 1971-72, about exactly the same thing, and, after further lengthy discussion, around 1978-79, it was decided simply and in principle that there would be a positive attitude towards an electoral strategy by Sinn Féin.

By sheer coincidence, Adams said, it was Britain's policy of criminalisation which caused the hunger-strikes that accelerated the process of electoral involvement. The victory of Bobby Sands made it easier to argue for an electoral strategy within republican ranks. The 1981 intervention by the prisoners in the twenty-six-county general election saw the success of two of their candidates, but it had been a mistake to enter the second election in February

1982. The difference between the two votes showed the difference between electoral interventions and electoral policy. In the six counties, there followed the Assembly and British general elections, with Sinn Féin victories which had caused external reverberations and a crisis that still continued.

The campaign needed to be built on a thirty-two-county basis, Adams said. 'If we were to develop our support in the twenty-six counties to even 50 per cent of our support in the six counties, the squeal that is coming out of Leinster House at the moment would become hysterical.' As in the North, in the South they must show up the contradictions in the state. They must show the people that they have rights, not just to a free Ireland, but to education, employment and homes as well.

Assassination Target

In March 1984 Adams and a number of his colleagues had to appear in the Belfast Magistrates court on a minor charge relating to the flying of a tricolour in a cortège on the night before his election. Adams was worried about the appearance for security reasons and had some colleagues survey the courts the day before his hearing and organise transport. On the morning of the court appearance Adams noticed a number of individuals there about whom he was quite suspicious and at the break for lunch the republicans asked that they be allowed stay in the building until the afternoon sessions began. However, this was not allowed for security reasons.

The group facing charges, Adams, Seán Keenan and Bob Murray, and two others, Joe Keenan and Kevin Rooney, who was driving, decided to go back to West Belfast to get some fish and chips. However, as they were driving along Howard Street, behind City Hall, in their gold-coloured Cortina, a car with three men in it drew alongside, and bullets showered the car.

Adams was sitting in the front passenger seat and was the main target of the gunmen. He did not see the attackers, but knew he was being shot at. He felt the thumps as the bullets hit him – one in the back of the neck, one in the left shoulder, two in the upper left arm. 'So this is what it is like,' he thought. About twenty shots were fired, nine of them hitting the car around the front passenger door. Murray, in the back seat, jumped to the floor. Seán Keenan got hit in the face and arm, Joe Keenan a number of times in the upper body and arms, and Kevin Rooney in the body. The shooting stopped as suddenly as it had started. 'Jesus Christ, I'm still alive,' whispered Adams to himself. They began to check each others' conditions.

Murray asked Adams if he was hit. 'Yes, a couple of times, but I'm OK,' he replied. Rooney, despite his injuries, kept driving, pressing on the car horn and breaking through any red traffic lights they met. The car reached the closed gates of the Royal Victoria Hospital, and Murray shouted for them to be opened. Adams, worried about the seriousness of Seán Keenan's wounds, said an Act of Contrition into his ear. Up at the hospital, Murray ran in and shouted that there were four shot men outside. Adams managed to walk in from the car, fighting to retain consciousness. All four were given emergency surgery.

The would-be assassins' car was trapped by an off-duty UDR man who had been driving in the area at the time and some plain clothes RUC men. The UDR man did a sudden U-turn and drove against the flow of traffic to intercept the gunmen, who were being chased by the RUC car. Two of the three gunmen were taken from their car at gunpoint. The third, who was bleeding badly (it later emerged that he had been hit by one of his own or his comrades' bullets) was left in the car; he was wounded in the shoulder and was later taken from the car and put lying on the pavement where he was given medical attention. His two comrades were held up against the railings. One was crying.

The paramilitary Ulster Freedom Fighters later claimed responsibility for the attack, accusing Adams of being the Chief-of-Staff of the IRA, responsible for 'the murderous campaign against Ulster'. Democratic Unionist Party Assemblyman George Seawright (later to be the victim of an assassin's bullet himself) said he regretted the attempt to kill Adams had not been successful. His colleague, the Revd William McCrea, said the 'removal' of Adams would have been a bonus for law and order. On the night of the shooting, there was widespread rioting in Belfast, and reports that loyalist paramilitaries had gone into hiding.

The bullet which had hit Adams in the neck had entered just below the hairline, crossed the neck without hitting the spine, and lodged in his right shoulder. It had come within millimetres of hitting his spine and leaving him paralysed. (The wound was to continue to cause him pain as did, to a lesser extent, one of the wounds in his upper left arm.) The surgeons removed three bullets from him, but another bullet remained in his arm. When, afterwards, Adams developed terrific pains in his upper left arm, which had developed a swelling, the doctors were of the opinion that it was shrapnel making its way to the surface, a normal process. The wound remained somewhat open and bits of the tweed jacket he had been wearing on the day of the shooting were being worked to the surface and emerging in the open wound. During the campaigning for the June EEC elections, the pain was becoming unbearable. What was happening was that a bullet – quite a large one, a .45mm – was slowly travelling around his arm, on occasion hitting the bone. He returned to the doctor and an X-ray revealed the bullet inside his swollen arm. The swelling was slit and the bullet removed. Its copper jacket had fractured and lead from the bullet had been entering his bloodstream.

At a press conference after his release from hospital, Adams said he believed British intelligence had advance knowledge about the assassination attempt. The follow-up operation to arrest the gunmen, the availability of plain clothes people in the area, contradictions in the version of events released by the RUC immediately after the shooting, all indicated clearly, he said, that the British wanted him and his colleagues killed and the 'added kudos of arresting those involved'.

Two years later the Belfast Magistrates court sentenced the three loyalist gunmen – Colin Grey (28), Gerald Walsh (43) and John Gregg (27), all from the Rathcoole area of Belfast, to sentences of 12 years for Gray and 18 years for the others. The judge said that a fourth man, who had organised the assassination attempt, was not in the court. It is believed in Belfast that this man, who had been in the courtroom on the morning of Adams' hearing and had aroused the suspicions of the republican group, had left his fellow gunmen after they had lost Adams' car in the traffic, but that the other three, quite by chance, had then found themselves up alongside the republicans' car and had opened fire. The charges against Adams and his colleagues, which had been the subject of the original court appearance were subsequently thrown out of court.

In April 1989 an application by Adams for compensation for the attack under the Criminal Injuries Act was rejected. A Crown lawyer told the Belfast court that the Northern Secretary had turned down the application because Adams had been a member of the IRA, was head of Sinn Féin which was an illegal though not a proscribed organisation, and because of his involvement in terrorism. Adams was not present in the court.

Punishments

One of the roles which the IRA had taken onto itself as its influence grew in areas of strong support was that of taking action against hooligans, criminals, and those guilty of sexual assault, whom the community would press the republicans to punish. The usual method of punishment was shots delivered to the limbs – a practice which came to be known as knee-capping. These punishments were usually given after warnings had been issued and ignored. Alternatively, offenders might have to humiliate themselves, perhaps by carrying placards apologising for their wrong-doing outside the church on Sunday or being tied to poles with their offences advertised on boards draped around their necks. The republicans disliked this sort of violence, which often left them open to strong condemnation by some community leaders. In May 1984 *An Phoblacht* carried an article which declared that it was now recognised that something more constructive than knee-capping and beating was required from the republican movement when dealing with 'hoods'. [6] United community action was needed. Not everyone is a hood, Adams was quoted as saying, but 'at the same time we must ensure that a stop is put to the anti-people activity of a minority which is having such an adverse effect on ordinary people'.

A week later the IRA shot dead a 'criminal' from the Divis Flats and wounded another from the Lower Falls area in both legs. In an interview in *An Phoblacht* the following September, an IRA spokesman said that the dead man, Jimmy Campbell, was the second man to be shot dead for 'criminal activities' in two years. He was a former member of the IRA, but had turned the training he had been given to criminal use (bank robbery), the IRA spokesman was quoted as saying.[7] Campbell had been wounded in punishment-shootings in the past, but had persisted with his activities. Around the time of the interview there had been a number of punishment beatings delivered by the IRA in the West Belfast area. The spokesman said that following the burst of heightened political awareness after the hunger-strikes, they had tried to 'refine' their methods away from punishment-shootings and beatings. 'The IRA would prefer not to be involved in punishments, but the community demands it,' he said.

An Injection of Reality

The July 1983 British general election had seen Sinn Féin increase its percentage of the total poll by over 3 per cent. The same election had seen the SDLP vote drop by almost 1 per cent of their poll in the Assembly elections. Now, as the EEC elections approached, republicans dreamed of – as others dreaded – the possibility of their winning a higher vote than the moderate nationalists. For Sinn Féin to be the voice of the nationalist majority in Northern Ireland, and to have a man who represented them sitting in a European Parliament, would be the final nail in British attempts to 'normalise' the six counties. For many in the movement who felt they were on an invincible roller-coaster, the EEC elections were to be another significant victory in their battle to reunite the island of Ireland.

Inside the northern steering committee which had been set up, Adams was arguing that the hype about outpolling the SDLP was too great, but his view was in the minority, with most of the committee opting to continue with the hype in the hope of squeezing the utmost out of their supporters.[8] By the day of the poll, the republican leadership believed they would not defeat Hume but it was decided not to say this to their followers. Some observers alleged that the reason Morrison, and not Adams, was put forward for the EEC election was precisely because they knew all along they could not win. To have Adams defeated would have been a greater psychological blow to the movement than to have Morrison beaten.

The EEC election was a difficult one for the republicans. The whole six counties was treated as one constituency, so they could not concentrate their resources in the areas where their support was strong. Nevertheless they fought a vigorous campaign, especially for a party which only three years previously had had its baptism of fire in contesting elections. The SDLP, conscious of the great importance of the contest, also fought a tough and skilful battle. It was thought afterwards that fear of the republicans overtaking the moderate nationalists spurred people to come out to vote for Hume.

Polling day was 14 June 1984 and after the votes were counted, Hume was announced to have won the nationalist seat. Morrison had won 91,476 votes, 11,125 less than had been won by the party in the general election of the previous year. The SDLP had survived. Hume was to represent the six counties in Strasbourg along with unionists the Revd Ian Paisley and John Taylor.

The Sinn Féin percentage vote, which had dropped only a tiny amount – from 13.4 per cent to 13.3 per cent – was still a significant one. But the illusion of the unstoppable republican bandwagon had been destroyed. Adams and the other members of the leadership, anticipating the SDLP victory, were quick to put forward positive interpretations of the outcome in an effort to dispel feelings of disillusionment. In the Republic, where Sinn Féin had contested the vote in all areas, the party had won only 2 per cent of the total vote.

In an interview later Adams said the results provided 'a useful injection of reality' for the party.[9] He took a positive attitude. In

Northern Ireland they had managed to hold onto their percentage of the vote, even though many people favoured Hume representing their interests in Europe. If it had been a matter of the national question, then more would have voted for Sinn Féin. Also, it was always hard to move a sitting representative, he said. He admitted that they had overworked the hype – 'our public position had to enthuse our workers and supporters'. He believed that the Hume vote would, in fact, lengthen the struggle. Some people who might have voted for Sinn Féin in 1983 might have found it difficult to tolerate some of the IRA's actions since then. 'I think there is a need to refer back to what I said at the 1983 Ard Fheis. That is, that revolutionary force must be controlled and disciplined so that it is clearly seen as a symbol of our people's resistance,' he said. He did not believe that the party had hit its 'ceiling' of support in the six counties and he still believed that it was possible for Sinn Féin to win the majority vote of the nationalist community. The 'real battle' would be seen next year, in the local elections, he added.

The low vote which Sinn Féin had received in the twenty-six counties was an indication of all that needed to be done. 'We fought the election for a number of reasons,' Adams said. 'As part of the process to end the isolation of republicans in that part of the country, to have a look at our organisation and to make it come into the real world. We have started an electoral strategy aimed at the local government elections next year.' The party would then be aiming to translate the EEC votes into council seats.

But while Adams was emphasising the electoral developments of the movement in his public utterances, others were reminding their supporters of the central role that violence played in their strategy. In a graveyard in Derry in June Martin McGuinness told the assembled crowd that the 'Irish Republican Army offers the only resolution to the present situation.... We recognise the value and the limitations of electoral success. We recognise that only disciplined revolutionary armed struggle by the IRA will ever end British rule'. He also reminded the IRA that 'armed struggle must be acceptable to the people on whose behalf it is carried out', and finished with an emotional declaration: 'Without the IRA we are on our knees. Without the IRA we are slaves. For fifteen years this generation of republicans have been off their knees. We will never be slaves again'.[10]

In an interview in August Adams again discussed the outcome of the EEC elections.[11] A republican base had existed in the North even before recent years, but such a base did not exist in the South.

All their support, on both sides of the border, was being given a party structure. The position in the South was mainly one of structure building at present, he said. Neither Dublin nor the SDLP were serious about Irish unity, he believed, and whereas he did not know if all the people in the six counties who were anti-unionist would ever come around to supporting the armed struggle, it was encumbent on Sinn Féin to give them an alternative to the SDLP. ('It could well be that we will not overtake the SDLP in the foreseeable future,' Morrison was to say later that year). [12] In the South, Adams said, the object would be to target those people who did not believe that the social and economic difficulties there could not be solved within a twenty-six-county context. The party would be aiming to win voters from Fianna Fáil and the Labour Party, but first there was a need to organise the party there.

In this interview Adams was also asked what he thought would come out of the London-Dublin talks which were then underway between the Thatcher and Fitzgerald governments, in an effort to find a way past the political impasse which once again existed in Northern Ireland and which was working to the advantage of Sinn Féin and to the disadvantage of the SDLP. He said that he viewed the talks as a process by which the British government could implement the strategy outlined in a British document on Ulster which had recently been drafted by T. E. Utley, John Biggs Davidson, Nicholas Budgen, Peter Lloyd and Patrick MacRory, entitled 'Britain's Undefended Frontier'. The document gave a number of suggestions for bringing the Republic into the greater British security operation against the IRA. 'They are talking about how to defeat republicanism,' Adams told his interviewer.

10: The SDLP looks for Help

Prior's Northern Assembly had been boycotted by the SDLP as it had been by Sinn Féin. The 'rolling devolution' envisaged by Prior, whereby the Assembly would be given ever greater powers as the representatives of both communities learned to work together, obviously could not occur without nationalist representatives taking part in the exercise. The running of Northern Ireland remained the responsibility of the London government, acting through its Secretary of State at the Northern Ireland Office at Stormont, Belfast. In Westminster the SDLP's tiny representation had little influence. In Northern Ireland it was a party without a parliament and in danger of becoming a party without relevance if some sort of political movement could not be initiated. Party leader John Hume began to call for a 'Council For a New Ireland' as early as before the 1982 elections for Prior's doomed Assembly. The object of the Council would be for nationalists to realistically assess how Ireland might be unified.

Out! Out! Out!

In May 1983 the Coalition government of the Republic announced the setting-up of the New Ireland Forum, in which all the major constitutional nationalist parties would come together to consider the unification of Ireland by constitutional methods, while ensuring the identity and interests of the Protestant community on the reunited island. The SDLP, the party of the constitutional nationalists in Northern Ireland, had been given a forum at which they could represent the interests of their constituents.

The New Ireland Forum brought together the Fianna Fáil, Fine Gael, SDLP and Labour parties, and it was openly admitted that the object was to act against the threat of Sinn Féin becoming the majority nationalist party in Northern Ireland and their claiming a legitimacy for IRA violence. Fitzgerald, in the opening speech of the Forum, said the parties were there to collectively reject 'murder, bombing and all the other cruelties that are being inflicted on the population of Northern Ireland in an attempt to secure political change by force. Let the men of violence take note of this unambiguous message from the nationalist people of Ireland: the future of Ireland will be built by the ballot box and the ballot box alone'.

The nationalist parties in Ireland were making perfectly clear their attitude to republican violence.

For a year and a half the Forum heard submissions and reports, but in the end it failed to come up with a single political model for consideration. Instead, the final Forum Report put forward three possibilities. The first was a unitary state, a thirty-two-county Ireland. This was the favoured option. The second was a federal or confederal arrangement, with both North and South having their own parliaments and executives, and both being under a national government which would hold the security brief. The third option was one whereby Northern Ireland would be the equal responsibility of the London and Dublin governments, who would share joint authority. Depressing economic forecasts for the three models put forward were dismissed in the final report.

In November 1984 at a summit meeting between Mrs Thatcher and Dr Fitzgerald, the Forum's conclusions were discussed, but the public statements to be made by the two leaders after the meeting were obviously not. Soon after the discussions ended, the Irish leader told journalists the report had been well received by the British premier. However, when Mrs Thatcher at a separate press conference was asked for her views on the three options in the report, her reply indicated that things were not as Dr Fitzgerald had thought. 'I have made it quite clear that a unified Ireland was one solution that is out. A second solution was confederation of two states. That is out. A third solution was joint authority. That is out.' Each time she put an emphasis on the word 'out' and her attitude to the Forum Report came to be summarised as 'Out! Out! Out!'.

Mrs Thatcher's reaction was a blow to the hopes of the SDLP and an encouragement to Sinn Féin. Again the SDLP had been made to look like an irrelevance as far as the aspirations of the nationalist population in Northern Ireland was concerned. This could only be of advantage to the republicans.

However, a passage in the Forum Report was to provide a seed from which would grow a new effort towards some sort of political movement in Northern Ireland. The passage referred to the need to deal with the 'alienation' of the northern nationalists from the security forces and the state in which they lived. The Irish Foreign Minister, Peter Barry, was calling for some way to end this alienation and the 'nationalist nightmare' in Northern Ireland. The point had been taken up by Secretary of State, James Prior, who began to push for greater recognition of the 'Irish identity' in Northern Ireland and for a system of communication with Dublin.

Officials from Dublin and London began talks about these issues in the month before Thatcher's blow to the efforts of the constitutional nationalists. Fitzgerald held his tongue after Mrs Thatcher's dismissal of the Forum's Report and the efforts centred on the talks continued.

The Undefended Frontier

Even before the 1981 hunger-strike was over the IRA had decided to try and kill Margaret Thatcher, the hatred of whom had grown steadily as the hunger-strikers died. On 15 September 1984 a friend of Adams', Patrick McGee, booked into Room 629 in the Grand Hotel in Brighton, under the pseudonym Roy Walsh. He planted a bomb behind the hardboard of the bath. During the Tory Party conference at that hotel a month later, on 12 October at just before 3am, the bomb exploded. Five people were killed and thirty injured. (The dead included one MP.) Mrs Thatcher had just moved from one room to another within her suite when the explosion occurred and only that saved her from death or serious injury. 'Thatcher,' the IRA said afterwards, 'will now realise that Britain cannot occupy our country, torture our prisoners and shoot our people on their own streets and get away with it. Today we were unlucky, but remember, we have only to be lucky once. You will have to be lucky always. Give Ireland peace and there will be no war.' However, the near-successful attempt on her life made the British premier all the more determined to defeat the IRA.

In his presidential speech at the November 1984 Ard Fheis, Adams spoke of the ongoing London-Dublin talks and again brought up the document 'Britain's Undefended Frontier; A Policy for Ulster'. He also touched on such issues as neutrality, foreign policy and the Kerry Babies' scandal, which had rocked the Republic that year. He sent messages of goodwill to republican prisoners and messages of solidarity to groups all over the world. He said that the Brighton bombing had been a 'blow for democracy', and that 'we in the public leadership of the republican struggle are the most likely victims of British assassination plans'. He attacked constitutional nationalism: 'In the Irish context it is a contradiction, when the constitutionality involved is British constitutionality, and British constitutionality in Ireland means the maintenance of a six-county colony which is not, never has been, and never will be, a viable social, political, or economic unit'. He did not mention the IRA throughout the entire address.

Adams saw the 'Undefended Frontier' document as guiding the

British-Irish talks that were taking place in 1984.[1] The document had been drawn up by the Independent Study Group and published the month before by the Institute for European Defence and Strategic Studies in London. The nationalist 'alienation' which existed in Northern Ireland was a danger to Dublin also, the report argued. There was a need for increased cross-border co-operation from Dublin, as an alternative to increased British repression in the North, which could in turn provoke a nationalist backlash throughout Ireland. The authors put forward the view that the ending of nationalist alienation could only be won by political concessions. They argued that co-operation from Dublin was vital to defeat the IRA and pointed to the IRA campaign in the 1950s, when the existence of internment on both sides of the border, with both governments united in their whole-hearted opposition to the IRA, had dealt decisively with the republicans. 'We think it should be made clear to the Dublin government that the degree of force which must be used in an attempt to restore order will be in inverse proportion to the degree of effective co-operation on security which can be achieved between the two governments.'

The authors recommended:
A joint London-Dublin security commission, including a military sub-committee made up of representatives of both armed forces;
A full-time secretariat drawn from Dublin and Whitehall civil servants;
London-Dublin summits at fixed intervals.

It was with fears of such developments that Adams watched the London-Dublin talks which centred on ending the 'nationalist nightmare'. In his 1984 Ard Fheis speech he appealed to the citizens of the Republic not to abandon 'their brothers and sisters' in the six counties.

Local Elections

In May 1985 Sinn Féin found itself once again back on the election trail in Northern Ireland. Adams had predicted the local elections to be the 'real battle' between the SDLP and the republicans, although since that comment in the wake of the EEC election results, more pessimistic talk had been coming from republican spokesmen. Neither Sinn Féin nor the SDLP were to contest all wards, with the moderate nationalists contesting more than the republicans. The campaigning was intense and when the votes were cast and the count finished, it emerged that a total of fifty-nine Sinn Féin councillors had been elected. It was a significant development and was to bring ongoing conflicts in local authority chambers across the six counties. But the total Sinn Féin vote had dropped 1 per cent on the 1984 EEC poll (though this might be accounted for by the fact that Sinn Féin was not competing in all areas). Nevertheless the republicans had failed to beat the moderates in the 'real battle': the SDLP won 113,967 votes to Sinn Féin's 75,685. Two weeks later, in what *An Phoblacht* described as 'an historic event', Sinn Féin councillor Seamus Kerr took the chair in the Omagh District Council on 28 May. He began his speech in Irish and bedlam erupted in the council chamber.

Meanwhile, in the twenty-six counties preparations for the coming local authority elections were underway. (Sinn Féin and The Workers' Party are the only political parties organised both north and south of the border.) Sinn Féin had twenty-eight local council seats – having first opted to contest and take local authority seats in the Republic in 1979 – and were hoping to improve on that number. Before the poll Adams said however that the real benefits would be in recruitment and organisation. As polling day approached in June Adams toured the twenty-six counties, joining his Sinn Féin colleagues as they canvassed.

The results saw a significant increase in the number of people voting for Sinn Féin since the 1979 local authority poll. But the figure was still small. In 1979 the party had won 29,798 votes, to elect twenty-eight members to thirty seats. The 1985 poll saw it winning 45,054 votes to elect thirty-six members to thirty-nine seats. It was an improvement but also an indication of the long way Sinn Féin had to travel before increasing its support in the Republic to significant levels.

Anglo-Irish Agreement

The London-Dublin talks continued, with the new Secretary of State, Douglas Hurd, taking over from James Prior. There was intensive speculation about the direction of the talks, especially among the unionists who were not being consulted at all. On 15 November 1985 the result of the year-long talks – the Anglo-Irish Agreement – was unveiled at a ceremony at Hillsborough Castle, Co. Down, attended by Mrs Thatcher and Dr Fitzgerald. A new permanent secretariat of civil servants from the two jurisdictions was established, as was a conference of ministers from both states with a brief to consider security and legal matters. A guarantee of the status of Northern Ireland as long as the majority there wished to remain in the UK formed a central part of the agreement, as did commitments to security-force co-operation in fighting terrorism, the prevention of discrimination and to a devolved power-sharing administration in the North. An inter-parliamentary tier, including members from both sovereign parliaments as well as Assembly members, was to be established. The agreement was an internationally recognised treaty between the two governments.

Adams viewed the Anglo-Irish Agreement as a triumph for the British in achieving the policies advocated by the authors of the 'Undefended Frontier' document. It addressed a problem outlined by a British army Brigadier in a 1978 report – British army intelligence could do nothing about the structure and organisation of the IRA in the twenty-six counties; only security force harmonisation could overcome this problem. The Agreement was designed to isolate and defeat republicans and, while it would not work, it would 'perpetuate the struggle' and make things worse in the long term, Adams said.[2] When the treaty was found not to work, then the British would introduce selective internment, pledges against violence for elected representatives and other measures, he predicted.

In a December interview with *An Phoblacht* Adams said one of the objectives of the Agreement was to re-establish Stormont, albeit in a modified form. 'Remember he [Hume] would be in Stormont now if Sinn Féin had not contested the Assembly elections.' Adams said that the developing adverse reaction by the unionists to the Agreement might well be one of the most far-reaching political developments in recent history. 'It could well change the relationship between unionists and the union.' In the same interview, he gave his view on one reason for IRA violence. 'IRA operations restate and underline the incorruptibility of the demand for Irish self-determination.'

Seamus Mallon, MP

While initially the reaction of the unionist leaders, Paisley and Molyneaux, did not seem to be one of complete opposition, the reaction of the people they represented soon had them declaring that the Anglo-Irish Agreement would have to be removed and that allowing Dublin government interference in the affairs of Northern Ireland, through the permanent secretariat, was an unacceptable affront to the North's sovereignty. In an action designed to display the extent of their opposition, the unionists resigned their Westminster seats in order to cause by-elections at which the indignation of the unionist people could be shown.

When the announcement was made, Adams put forward the idea of a nationalist boycott of the elections, being partly spurred by a fear that the SDLP would win an increased percentage of the vote. The boycott was rejected and Sinn Féin opted to contest four of the fifteen constituencies affected by the resignations, with Jim McAllister, Danny Morrison, Owen Carron and Frank McDowell going forward. Adams said before polling day that if the SDLP had come to an electoral agreement with the republicans, then nationalists could have taken four of the vacated seats. In the event, the nationalists managed to take one seat from the unionists, with the SDLP deputy leader Seamus Mallon taking the Newry/Armagh seat. The Sinn Féin vote in the constituencies they contested was down on the general elections results. The constitutional nationalists had improved their position with the winning of the Anglo-Irish Accord.

Abstentionism

At the 1985 Ard Fheis the Sinn Féin delegates voted on a motion that the policy of abstentionism from Dáil Éireann, the southern parliament, be treated as a matter of tactics rather than principle. Two years earlier, when Adams was elected President, delegates had voted out a rule that discussion of abstentionism be prohibited at future conferences. Now, in 1985, the issue of abstentionism was to be taken one step further. Adams took no public position on the issue, not least because of his statement only two years previously at the Ard Fheis when he said his appointment as President did not mean he was going to lead the party into the Dáil.

However, he had already decided that the party would have to abandon this policy, and later gave his reasoning:

A large part of the nationalist and republican population in the 6 counties regards abstentionism as posing no problems in terms of giving their votes because they do not see participation in the institutions of the state as having anything to offer them. But in the 26 counties, while people may be very scornful of the performance of their politicians and cynical about the institutions of the state, they nevertheless expect the people they elect to represent them in these institutions. [3]

Adams, too, had his sights on the South of Ireland. British efforts to win that state to its side were not going to go uncontested.

However at the 1985 Ard Fheis there was a danger that some elements of the organisation, who held that the principle of abstentionism was one of the unalterable tenets of republicanism, would react so strongly against any attempts to undermine the principle that they might split the organisation. In order to head off a direct confrontation the issue was couched in terms of whether abstentionism was a principle or a tactic. If the delegates voted that it was solely a tactic, then in time the leadership believed they could convince the membership that taking seats in Leinster House was the best tactic. For policy to be changed the vote had to be by a two-thirds majority. Either way, the vote would show the level of resistance which existed and also identify it.

During the debate Morrison reminded the delegates that the IRA had voiced its support for the development of electoral intervention and pledged that there would be no winding-down of the armed struggle. The issue was not that there be a change of policy, he said, but simply that abstentionism be seen as a tactic. When the vote came, a majority voted that abstentionism be seen as a tactic, but not sufficient a majority to change policy. Nevertheless it was an encouraging result and the leadership now set about preparing for the next year's Ard Fheis, by which time they hoped to have the ground prepared for the acceptance of ending abstentionism in the Republic.

Revolt

In February 1986 Adams travelled to Holland to visit Brendan McFarlane and Gerard Kelly, who were being held in jail while fighting an (ultimately successful) extradition application from Britain. MacFarlane had led an escape from the Maze in September 1983, in which he and thirty-seven others managed to break out, and nineteen in all managed to evade immediate recapture. It was a major achievement for the republicans, and a major embarrassment for the British. The escape was the largest in Europe since the Second World War. But in January 1986 MacFarlane and Kelly were arrested in a flat in Holland, apparently on an arms-buying expedition. After visiting them in prison, Adams said their conditions were very harsh, and that they were being held in virtual solitary confinement. A man Adams met while in Holland offered him use of his Paris flat and the republican leader spent a week away from the pressures of Northern Ireland, getting up every day to walk the streets of Paris, relishing the beauty of the buildings and parks and the feeling of peace and relative safety.

Meanwhile however, within the ranks of the IRA a similar contest to the one taking place within Sinn Féin over the development of the organisation was underway, with a number of senior and experienced volunteers unhappy with the growing emphasis on electoral politics which they believed was taking from the 'war effort'. These dissenters began to press for the holding of an Army Convention – an unusual request. This would entail a meeting of delegates from all IRA formations in order to elect a new executive. In 'times of war' the IRA was usually run by the executive which in turn selected the members of the army council, which was in charge of running the overall military campaign. The last convention had been in 1970, and the calling for a new one was an expression of dissatisfaction with the direction the organisation was taking, and with the leadership.

Four senior northern members of the IRA were prominent in the push for the Army Convention and for a return to an all-out campaign. They were against the concentration of so much of the movement's resources in the Sinn Féin political machine, feeling that more should be devoted to the war effort and to paying volunteers. There were feelings that the Belfast Brigade was not active enough and hints of dissatisfaction with the OC of the Brigade.

The canvassing for a convention was dealt with quickly by the leadership. Members who had been canvassed for support were interviewed and made to swear statements. The four senior northern dissenters were expelled from the IRA in early 1985 and told they would be assassinated if they joined a rival organisation. The expulsions did not eradicate the pressure for an Army Convention, but it gave the leadership time to secure their position.

A friend of Adams was later to grow disaffected and leave the movement because of the direction in which Adams was bringing it. Bob Murray, the only man to have escaped injury during the attempted assassination of Adams, wrote a letter to a Belfast newspaper, saying the abstentionism debate was like seeing history repeat itself.[4]

'Are we once again to witness the classic counter-revolutionary tactic in action?' wrote Murray. 'Leaders can be wrong and very often are. Four years ago I remember Gerry Adams saying "when you talk about constitutional politics in an Irish context, it is British constitutionalism to which you refer". What happened Gerry? Where did it go wrong? What changed? Where and when did it change, or had the decisions already been taken, even then, as your oration at Bodenstown ... would suggest?'

In the months before the Army Convention, Adams and his supporters worked hard on winning support from the militant wing for the direction he was taking the movement. The level of IRA activity increased. There were also changes in the command structure of the Belfast Brigade and a promise to drop the 'woman's right to choose' position on the abortion issue. Adams appeared at a number of old IRA gatherings to reinforce his affinity with the old traditions. It was in the middle of all this canvassing that unionist MPs resigned over the Anglo-Irish Agreement and the SDLP's Seamus Mallon won his Westminster seat.

The Convention was held on 20 September 1986 and *An Phoblacht* later carried an IRA statement which provided Adams with his strongest weapon for the pending Ard Fheis. The statement began with a rededication to, and an expression of confidence in, the armed struggle as a means of breaking the British connection. Two resolutions had been passed, the statement read, that changed sections of the constitution of Óglaigh na hÉireann (the IRA) in ways that directly affected electoral strategy in the Republic. The ban on volunteers discussing or advocating the taking of parliamentary seats in Dáil Éireann had been removed, and the ban on supporting republicans who take their seats, was also removed.

When the 600 or so Sinn Féin delegates filed into Dublin's Mansion House on 1 November, they were aware that what was to happen at that year's Ard Fheis would be a milestone in republican history. In his Presidential Address Adams appealed to the membership not to split over the abstentionism issue. If the vote was against the ending of abstentionism, then he would continue to work with the republican movement as always, he said (though he added later that if abstentionism remained then 'your leadership is going to be back here year after year until it has convinced you of this necessity'). He said that abstentionism was 'merely a deeply rooted and emotive symptom of the lack of republican politics and the failure of successive generations of republicans to grasp the centrality, the primacy, and the fundamental need for republican politics. This truth must be grasped. It is a difficult one for many to accept given the conspiratorial and repressive nature of our past, our distrust for "politics and politicians" and a belief that "politics" is inherently corrupt. But once it is grasped then everything else follows logically, especially the need to develop our struggle at the level of peoples understanding'.

During the entry to politics of nationalists Gerry Fitt, Paddy Devlin, or Paddy Kennedy, he had been opposed to the republican support, or even the standing aside, which had assisted these people, he said. Removing abstentionism would 'initiate an increase in our party membership and could change the political complexion of the party', but there was a need to 'keep our republican gut', ie not forget the objective of the republican movement – Irish unity.

Adams' strongest card was the backing of the IRA. 'The decisions of the General Army Convention are not binding on Sinn Féin Ard Fheiseanna, but the logic of those who would consider withdrawing support from Sinn Féin if we change the abstentionist policy must be applied also to your attitude to the army. And the logic which would dictate withdrawal of support from Sinn Féin if decisions go against you means that you have already decided to withdraw solidarity and support from the IRA and the armed struggle.'

What was happening in 1986 was completely different from what had happened in 1970; this time the men of violence were on the side of the developing political strategy.

Martin McGuinness put the dispute within the movement in more personal terms in an address to the delegates. He began with a commitment that the leadership had absolutely no intention of going into Westminster or Stormont, and a denial that if Sinn Féin entered Leinster House the war would be wound-down. 'This Ard Fheis,' he said, 'and you, the delegates, deserve to know the whole story of this debate. In fact, what you're witnessing here is not a debate over one issue, but two – abstentionism and the leadership of the republican struggle. The two issues should not be confused and those who are considering leaving along with the members of the former leadership should consider carefully what I am about to say. The reality is that the former leadership of this movement has never come to terms with this leadership's criticism of the disgraceful attitude adopted by them during the disastrous 18-month ceasefire in the mid-'70s. Instead of accepting the validity of our case, as others who have remained have done, they chose to withhold their wholehearted support from the leadership which replaced them.'

He finished with a plea to those considering walking out if there was a vote in favour of ending abstentionism. 'If you allow yourself to be led out of this hall today, the only place you are going – is home. You will be walking away from the struggle. Don't go my friends. We will lead you to the republic.'

The motion being voted upon was a lot more straightforward than that of 1985, reflecting the leadership's increased confidence. When the vote was taken, 429 of the delegates voted to end abstentionism; 161 voted to retain it. When the vote became known, Ruairí Ó Brádaigh and Daithí Ó Connaill stood up at the bottom of the hall and marched out, followed by a number of supporters. They assembled at a hotel just outside Dublin and held a press conference in front of a banner reading 'Republican Sinn Féin'. Back at the Mansion House, it had been decided to register Sinn Féin as a political party at Leinster House and that the 'woman's right to choose' policy on abortion be dropped.

At the end of the month Adams was interviewed in *An Phoblacht*.[5] The difference between the Dáil and other parliaments, he said, was that the people in the twenty-six counties accepted the Dáil, whereas the people in the six counties did not accept the British parliament. Now, for the first time in sixty years, republicans in the twenty-six counties had a clear role. Hard graft by republicans in the twenty-six counties would be the seed from which – nurtured by some unknown future event – the revolution would break out.

The Politics of Irish Freedom

At the end of 1986 a book by Adams, *The Politics of Irish Freedom*, was published. It was not, he said, an account of republican politics but rather a personal statement. The book begins with an excerpt from a poem by Bobby Sands, 'The Rhythm of Time':

> There's an inner thing in every man,
> Do you know this thing my friend?
> It has withstood the blows of a million years,
> And will do so to the end...
>
> It lights the dark of this prison cell,
> It thunders forth its might,
> It is the undauntable thought, my friend,
> That thought that says 'I'm right!

In *The Politics of Irish Freedom* Adams gives the republican view of events leading up to the eruption of violence in Northern Ireland in 1969, and of subsequent British strategies ever since right up to the 1985 Anglo-Irish Agreement. He repeats the view that it is only when the British leave Ireland that peace will come and that loyalists will be 'pragmatic' if the British withdraw. To the charge that the IRA is sectarian, he replies that given its resources and ability to mount operations against the security forces, its members would be able to slaughter ordinary Protestants if they so wished, but have not done so. Also, it was the British who decided to withdraw thousands of troops and 'Ulsterise' the war, getting one section of the community to fight for them. Indeed, he sees anti-sectarianism as an important facet of republicanism along with separatism, secularism, nationalism and a radical social dimension.

The ills of the twenty-six counties, he argues, are due to the existence of Northern Ireland. Those concerned with poverty in the twenty-six counties should be struggling for a united Ireland. Real national independence is the prerequisite for socialism, he writes. The South is an economy being run by an agent class, working for foreign, mainly British interests. Partition cut off the vital industrial base in the six counties and the important port of Belfast. But for the agents who run the foreign-capital-dominated economy in the twenty-six counties, attempts to end partition are against their interests and so against the interests of the Establishment. Meanwhile, the economy has been unable to develop properly, at a great social cost made manifest in unemployment and emigration. The six counties in the North are a tiny economic enclave on the fringe of the British economy, without any powers of economic development or initiative. 'While the British retain control the six counties will suffer further de-industrialisation and greater dependency on the politically motivated hand-outs from Britain,' he writes.

Less often heard views are included in the chapter on culture, which Adams says 'forms a major part of the conquest of Ireland'. He quotes from Pearse's analysis of the Irish education system, *The Murder Machine*:

> The system has aimed at the substitution for men and women of mere things... Things have no allegiance. Like other things the are for sale... There is no education system in Ireland.

Education should inspire, but instead it tames. Adams puts a strong emphasis on the role of language in the British conquest of Ireland, and on the republican effort to reconquer it. Culture is the 'totality of our response to the world we live in', and language is the means by which this culture is communicated. When a language is lost then the shared history and experience of a people which that language contained is also lost. He outlines the nature of the fifth century Brehon laws and argues that it was a culture which included a communal attitude and a 'welfare state' attitude which was destroyed by the British.

'It is capitalistic ideas, feudalism and the concept of private property which have been imported into Ireland, not socialist ideas,' he writes. Once again, as he did by using James Connolly, Fintan Lalor and the First Dáil to argue for a radical social pro-gramme as part of republicanism, by using Irish history and the resentment of the British role in Irish history to argue for a socialist society in Ireland, he is making it difficult for the traditionalist, conservative element within republicanism to argue against his 'foreign ideas'.

Adams writes that the culture now being fostered in Ireland reflects the politics, economics, values, attitudes, aspirations and thoughts of 'our rulers' – the British and other imperialist forces. It is a dependency culture which manifests itself in both parts of Ireland as resistance to change, a lack of national pride, a feeling of national inferiority and in begrudgery. It leads to an acceptance of the failure of both Irish states, and of a 'no-hope future'. He quotes the late Martín Ó Cadhain, the former 'IRA activist, professor, and writer'. 'Tosóidh athghabháil na hÉireann le hathgabháil na Gaeilge.' (The reconquest of Ireland will begin with the reconquest of the Irish language.) The truth of this has been recognised by the British, who have moved quickly to undermine attempts by Sinn Féin to foster the Irish language. A language revival is underway among the working-class people of Belfast, he writes, and the minds of the people there are more free than those of their fellow Irish citizens in the twenty-six counties. He calls on revolutionary republicans to educate themselves about the centrality of the question of cultural resistance to the fight for the reconquest of all Ireland.

'As Padraig Pearse said of the Gaelic League, the Easter Rising of 1916 was assured from the moment the League was founded,' he writes. 'The Irish language is the reconquest of Ireland and the reconquest of Ireland is the Irish language.' The alternative is a 'dustbin of Anglo-American culture', leaving the Irish worse off morally, psychologically, intellectually and materially. The final section of the book looks at Sinn Féin and the prospect of peace in Ireland. 'The philosophers and thinkers of the 1916 Rising did not survive it, and this set the stage for counter-revolution,' he writes. But now, for Sinn Féin, the radical tendency is again, for the first time in recent history, in control.

11: 'Undiluted Fascism'

Less than a year after the historic Ard Fheis vote removing abstentionism, Sinn Féin was involved in its first general election without
abstention in the Republic. The Fine Gael/Labour coalition disin-
tegrated and Taoiseach Garret Fitzgerald dissolved his government, setting a date of 17 February 1987 for the poll. The issue that
dominated the contest was the economy, centring around the
crises of high income taxes, unemployment, emigration and the
national debt. In the newspapers and on television (where Sinn Féin
were banned under Section 31 of the Republic's Broadcasting Act)
the republicans received little attention. The party had opted to
field twenty-seven candidates in twenty-four constituencies and its
party machinery went into overdrive throughout the Republic in
the fight for votes. In Dublin, the party set up a 'pirate' radio station
which broadcast republican propaganda and occasional pop songs
and ballads, in an attempt to overcome the Section 31 censorship.
Adams himself toured the country, joining the candidates as they
canvassed in their constituencies. Fitzgerald denounced him as 'an
evil man'.

Early in the campaign, Adams declared that Sinn Féin did not
expect to win a seat. The second election after the dropping of
abstentionism would be the first true indicator of the effect that
policy change had had and show the success or otherwise that the
party was having in building up its base. Once again, he was saying
that the contest was more important for the winning of new
members and the overall development of the organisation. He also
said that if the election meant nothing else, it meant 'an end to
republican elitism'.

When the election results were announced, they showed that
Adams had been correct in his caution, though the poll was even
worse for the republicans than they had been estimating. The
electorate in the twenty-six counties was concerned with 'bread
and butter' issues and Sinn Féin was deemed irrelevant. Party
spokespeople made little effort to hide their disappointment afterwards. Even in the border areas where two H-Block prisoner
TDs had been elected during the hunger-strike, the party failed to
poll well. In Cavan/Monaghan, Caoimhgháin Ó Caoláin came
sixth in the list of contenders; in Louth, Arthur Morgan came ninth.

However the votes won by Christy Burke in the impoverished Dublin Central constituency gave some encouragement. His vote had increased from 1,500 in the November 1982 poll, to 2,300 in the 1983 by-election, to 2,500 in the 1985 poll.

Adams had spent the count at Cootehill, in Co. Cavan, to witness Caoimhghán Ó Caoláin's disappointing poll. 'The director of elections believed we would get 3 per cent and hoped for 5 per cent,' Adams said in an interview afterwards. In fact, the party had won just 32,933 votes, or 1.85 per cent of the poll. (Following the election, Fianna Fáil, which had failed to win a majority of seats, managed to form a minority government which, with the support of the opposition Fine Gael party, began to implement a programme of public service cuts designed to allow them stabilise the national debt.) 'I never thought we were going to win a seat. It will take some time for that to happen,' said Adams.[1] There were no easy options. Only hard work of 'the most mundane and tedious nature, intelligent planning, patience and involvement on a daily basis with the electorate will lead to the electoral gains we require'. What was needed now was that lessons learned be acted upon, local organisation consolidated, recruitment stepped up, local press contacts maintained and links made with local people developed. A week later Adams gave his analysis of the outcome:

> With a great deal of hindsight, I am sorry that abstentionism wasn't dropped years ago. High points of national discontent in the last 20 years could have been properly consolidated and developed by a radical, non-abstentionist Sinn Féin organisation. We missed those opportunities and allowed the Dublin government to forge ahead with its strategy of revisionism, partitionism, and black propaganda. That mistake will never be made again by us.

Loughgall Ambush

On Saturday morning, 25 April 1987, the second highest judge in Northern Ireland, and one particularly hated by the IRA, Lord Justice Maurice Gibson (73) and his wife Cecily were killed instantly when they were caught in a bomb blast seconds after they drove through the border crossing at Killeen, Co. Armagh. The couple had arrived in Dublin from Liverpool that morning and been given a garda escort to the border. There they shook hands with the escort and were driving along a mile-long stretch of road just inside the border, towards where the RUC were waiting at the end of the road, when the IRA bomb hidden at the roadside was detonated. Lord Gibson had presided over the trial of a number of

RUC members involved in the killings of three IRA men in 1982, deaths which gave rise to the 'shoot-to-kill' controversy, later investigated by Manchester Deputy Chief Constable, John Stalker. Lord Justice Gibson had dismissed the case and commended the men for sending the republicans 'to the final court of justice'.

Less than two weeks later the Provisionals, who were jubilant with their success in killing such a senior member of the judiciary, received what was the greatest single blow to the IRA since the war with the 'Black and Tans' over sixty years earlier. On the evening of Thursday, 8 May, an eight-man IRA unit (which included a number of experienced republican fighters, led by veteran gunman and former Sinn Féin councillor Jim Lynagh, from Monaghan) set out to destroy the part-time RUC station at Loughgall, Co. Armagh. Using a JCB digger to carry the bomb, the unit managed to blow up the station, but as they were about to make their escape in a Hiace van, a squad of SAS men and specially trained RUC men, who had been lying in wait for the republicans, cut them down in a massive hail of bullets. All eight IRA men were killed. A civilian, Anthony Hughes, who was in a car with his brother and some hundred yards from the site of the ambush during the shooting, was also killed when their car was showered with bullets by the security forces. Mr Hughes died instantly and his brother was seriously injured.

The deaths caused a numbness and a seething anger among republicans, but gave rise to satisfaction among hardline unionists. The Revd Ian Paisley praised the security forces. The OUP leader, James Molyneaux, said he hoped there would be no allegations of 'shoot-to-kill' policies. The answer to that charge, he said, was that 'terrorists ought not to be driving a bomb into an RUC station'.

Jim Lynagh, from Monaghan, was 31 when he was killed. He had been in the IRA since his teens and was a popular and admired activist. The security forces regarded him as one of their main targets along the border area and he was credited with a large number of IRA operations. He had been injured and imprisoned, but had always returned to the IRA. His obituary in *An Phoblacht* said that after being released from prison he had contacted the IRA before contacting his family. It also said he had known his time would come sooner rather than later.

Adams delivered the oration at his funeral. Lynagh, he said, 'would not have complained about the enemy action. He probably would have thought that they did not have to shoot some of the younger volunteers (Seamus Donnelly was 19 and Declan Arthurs 21 when they died in the ambush) but he wouldn't have complained. He knew the risks. He did not have to cross the border'. For Adams, he had fought and given his life for Irish freedom. He finished his oration by saying that Loughgall 'will become a tombstone for British policy in Ireland, and a bloody milestone in the struggle for freedom, justice and peace'.[2]

At the funeral of Tony Gormley, from Galbally, Co. Tyrone, another of the ill-fated IRA unit, Adams warned that the republican movement 'would avenge the deaths of the eight IRA members'. Adams addressed the mourners in the small churchyard in Aughnagar, near Dungannon, just as the British government was announcing a general election for June. 'Margaret Thatcher and Tom King and all the other rich and powerful people will be sorry in their time for what happened in Loughgall,' he said and his words were interpreted by the newspapers as a threat on the lives of politicians. The killings were a severe blow to the IRA, he said. 'We will remember Tony Gormley and we will remember Loughgall.'[3]

McGuinness, speaking at the funeral of Paddy Kelly (30) the leader of the East Tyrone Brigade, vowed that out of the hatred created by the killings 'will come a greater strength as the British themselves will see, a greater number of IRA recruits, not just in Tyrone but throughout the Six Counties'.

Election Again

Sinn Féin contested the 1987 British elections with the slogan 'Freedom, Justice, Peace', and threw itself vigorously into the campaign. On the eve of the poll John Hume said that the electorate had 'sensed the historical importance of a major electoral breakthrough' for the SDLP. The Anglo-Irish Agreement had broken the old moulds and opened the way for new political options, he said. Adams, in turn, claimed that his was now the only nationalist party and that the Sinn Féin vote would hold and would rise in West Belfast. More, he said, could be achieved for the people of Ireland outside the British parliament than in it. Polling day was 11 June and in both Ireland and Britain observers waited anxiously to see how the two sides were faring in the contest for the support of the nationalist community in Northern Ireland. The result of the poll in Britain was known within hours of the polling booths closing – Thatcher had been returned to power once again, making her one of the longest serving British Prime Minister's ever. But those awaiting the Northern Ireland poll had to wait until late the following day.

The result proved to be another depressing one for the republicans. Their vote had fallen since the 1983 general election, while the SDLP poll had risen. It looked like a triumph for the party of the Anglo-Irish Agreement. Sinn Féin's percentage of the vote had dropped by just over 2 per cent, to 11.3 per cent, while that of the SDLP had risen by just over 3 per cent, to 21 per cent. The republicans were losing the battle for the majority nationalist vote. Morrison, who four years earlier had come so close to winning a seat, had his vote fall by 3,500. In Derry, McGuinness's vote fell also. The SDLP representation had jumped from one seat to three seats, with Seamus Mallon holding his seat and Eddie McGrady winning the South Down contest.

Adams' vote, however, increased, though only marginally. He won 16,862 votes, over 440 more than four years previously. Asked if he would be taking his seat, he replied, 'I think Guy Fawkes had the right idea about parliament'. He told newspaper reporters the Sinn Féin vote was holding and this showed the party had not been marginalised by the Anglo-Irish Agreement. When he began his acceptance speech in Irish in Belfast City Hall, a heckler shouted, 'No one can understand you, Gerry!' He gave a brief address, and accused his opponents of fighting a dirty campaign.

Afterwards, he was carried down the stairs of the municipal building as loyalists at the top shouted, 'Murderers! Murderers! Murderers!', to which the Sinn Féin supporters replied, 'I-I, I-R-A! I-I, I-R-A!', and waved their fists in the air. Adams was bundled into a black taxi and as the republican cortège began to make its way out onto the street, the loyalist gang banged on the cars and shouted, 'Remember Loughgall'. One loyalist youth had a placard draped around him, which read, 'Gerry, we invite you to a party in Loughgall tonight. Bring eight friends, that is if you're brave enough for a party'. The republican cars made their way out past the shouting, kicking crowd. The last car accelerated and screeched out through the crowd and was chased by some RUC men. They caught up with the car at nearby traffic lights, where they jumped on it, dragged its occupants out, and hauled them off to the police station. A car window was smashed and the car impounded.

In the following week's issue of *An Phoblacht*, the large front page headline read 'Sinn Féin Here to Stay', and stood beside a picture of Adams. Consolidation in the North – rather than overtaking the SDLP – was now considered an achievement. The party sights were being lowered.

Operation Mallard

At the end of October 1987 two experienced IRA men were transporting a bomb in Derry when it exploded. The men, Paddy Deery and Eddie McShaffrey, were rushed to hospital, but were dead on arrival. Local people set fire to the hijacked car in which the men had been travelling, before it could be forensically examined by the police. That weekend the Sinn Féin Ard Fheis took place in Dublin, clouded by the latest deaths, the deaths at Loughgall and a general run of bad luck and tragedy which seemed to be dogging the movement. There were no contentious motions to be fought over and in his presidential address Adams devoted most of his time to attacking the Dublin government, Section 31, the cuts in public service expenditure, unemployment and extradition. The February election results had shown the enormity of the task which faced Sinn Féin in the twenty-six counties, he said, and the party would have to agitate around the issues of unemployment and extradition. The greatest political advance of recent times had been the fall of Stormont, but the Anglo-Irish Agreement had as one of its objectives the resurrection of a partitionist arrangement and administration. The Agreement itself was now part of the nationalist nightmare.

He finished with mention of Loughgall. The British had tried to smash the morale of the entire IRA by their wipeout at Loughgall, he said. Eight volunteers had been killed; but the republicans would not be defeated. 'We have right on our side.'

On the Monday after the Ard Fheis, Adams gave a brief oration at the funerals in Derry of the two IRA men who had died the previous Wednesday. There had been awful scenes of fighting at the funeral of IRA man Larry Marley earlier that year and again at the Derry funerals there was a large, ostentatious turn out by the security forces. Fighting broke out during which one of the two coffins fell from the hands of the pallbearers onto the pavement.

That weekend news had emerged about the capture of an enormous arms cargo on board the Irish boat the *Eksund*, which had been arrested by French customs. The massive cargo had been on route from Libya to Ireland and included 1,000 Kalashnikov rifles, ground to air missiles, grenades, grenade launchers and two tons of plastic explosives. It was more like the kind of munitions a conventional army would require, not a small, tight guerrilla force. What was more surprising was that intelligence strongly indicated that a similar, or perhaps even larger cargo of arms and explosives, had been landed in the Republic before the capture of the *Eksund*.

The following Sunday an IRA bomb blasted through a Remembrance Day ceremony in Co. Fermanagh, dealing yet another severe blow to the republican movement. The bomb was placed at the bottom of the gable wall of St Michael's community centre at Enniskillen and was detonated at 10.40am, a quarter of an hour before the Remembrance Day ceremony was due to begin. An iron barrier which prevented people from crossing the road at this dangerous bend, lined the kerb that ran along parallel to the gable wall. On 8 November this barrier was acting as a crash barrier, keeping the civilian spectators back from the procession. When the bomb exploded, the barrier prevented the crowd being thrown out by its force. They were hemmed in and the wall of the old community centre fell on top of them. Eleven were killed and sixty-three injured. All the dead were Protestants.

One of the eleven to die was a young nurse, Marie Wilson, who had spent her short professional life treating the sick as a student nurse at the Royal Victoria Hospital in West Belfast. An account of her dying moments by her father, Gordon, was broadcast to the world and painted a picture of family love that contrasted hugely with the intent – whatever exactly that intent was – of the bombers. 'I love you daddy,' she had said as she lay dying beneath the rubble. And then: 'I'm frightened.'

Later her father said that he bore 'no ill will. That sort of talk is not going to bring her back to life. She was a great wee lassie. She loved her profession. She was a pet and she's dead. She's in heaven and we'll meet again'. His words of love and forgiveness rocked Ireland and the world. Thousands filed through the Mansion House in Dublin (where the Sinn Féin Ard Fheiseanna are held) to sign a book of condolences.

'The IRA made a terrible mistake at Enniskillen,' Adams said in an interview in *An Phoblacht* eleven days later.[4] The dignity of the relatives of the victims in their mourning, their forgiveness, and especially the words of Gordon Wilson, 'had a deep effect on me and I am sure on other republicans', Adams stated. He emphasised that every IRA unit must realise that he or she has the capacity to advance or retard the nationalist struggle. Concern for civilians must be a key factor in the IRA's deliberations. The people's revulsion was now being manipulated into anti-republicanism and the Enniskillen tragedy was being used in an attempt to invalidate the entire struggle, he said. Internment was now a live issue and if introduced, would be on a thirty-two-county basis. Tragedy was being used to expedite the introduction of increased repression. It was too soon to say what the effect of the bombing on the 'base' was, but it was clear that 'efforts to broaden the base have most certainly been upset'. All in all, he continued, 'we are in for a difficult period'. He finished by saying that the tragedy had to be seen in the context of Britain's claim to Ireland.

In a later interview in *The Irish Press*, he said that the bombing had dealt a 'body blow' to his party's hopes of expanding its support base in the Republic.[5] In that same interview Adams' own vulnerability and the attempt on his life were raised by the interviewer. 'I've known hundreds – hundreds – of close friends die in the last seventeen years. I've known hundreds of widows and orphaned children. I have a nodding acquaintance at least with 80 per cent of Republican prisoners, and am close to scores of them. We live permanently under pressure in West Belfast so it didn't take being shot at to remind me of all that this conflict means,' he replied.

Following the bomb the IRA claimed that the radio-controlled detonator was activated by the British Army's bomb detection equipment, but this was denied by the security forces. Reports contradicting the IRA version of events later emerged, stating the bomb was detonated by a timer device. The unit involved was later to be disciplined by the IRA following additional outrages, including the murder of an ex-RUC man in Co. Donegal.

The massive wave of revulsion following the Enniskillen bombing did the republicans huge damage in the twenty-six counties and introduced a new political climate. The horror of the bombing coupled with reports on the size of the *Eksund* cargo and the news that similarly sized cargoes had already been landed increased many people's fear of the republican paramilitaries and the havoc which they might bring to the entire island. A new Extradition Act, which allowed for the extradition of wanted Irish citizens to Britain even in cases of what might be termed as 'political crimes', was being introduced in the twenty-six counties and the tragedy speeded its arrival.

On Monday, 23 November, the Irish government, working with the security forces in the North, launched a massive security operation in the Republic which was dubbed 'Operation Mallard'. The massive countrywide search for republican arms dumps was launched by the Minister for Justice, Gerry Collins, who said the arms which the IRA now held 'threatened the very existence of the state'. While the search was initially unsuccessful in unearthing the massive munitions which the security forces believed the IRA were storing, it did however have a 'scare-factor', worrying thousands of

Irish citizens and making them fear and react against the IRA. From the republican perspective, it was seen as massive harassment and intimidation by the southern security forces.

Justice and Peace

Just two months after the horrific Enniskillen bombing Gerry Adams and John Hume both received a letter from a third party, who wished to remain anonymous, suggesting they meet and talk 'to explore whether there could be agreement on an overall nationalist political strategy for justice and peace'. For Adams and Sinn Féin, suffering intense vilification and isolation, the invitation offered an avenue back towards the semi-respectability which they had enjoyed prior to the November massacre, as well as an opportunity for constructive debate. For Hume, this very point meant he was to come in for some trenchant criticism.

Adams brought the letter to the party Ard Comhairle, which welcomed the opportunity and set up a monitoring committee to handle details of the talks. A fascinating debate was to begin between the two principal nationalist leaders in Northern Ireland. It would be an attempt by Hume, one of the sharpest political minds in Ireland, to expose as wrong the political analysis which Adams had developed and, therefore, to undermine his assertion that the republican 'armed struggle' was justifiable. On 11 January 1988 the two had their first meeting, a private session which lasted several hours and during which they exchanged their analyses of the political problem in Northern Ireland and the shape which any discussion between their two parties should take. When the news of the meeting reached the media, there was a thunder of condemnation from loyalist and British politicians, and expressions of worried doubt from representatives south of the border. It was alleged that Hume had thrown the republicans a political lifeline. On the other hand, others registered their unease with the talks, but said they had faith in Hume's political judgment.

The two sides exchanged documents on 17 March and delegations, led by Adams and Hume, met to discuss the content of the papers on 23 March. Sinn Féin, in their document, had stressed that the role of the British in the affairs of Northern Ireland was not neutral, and was in fact malign. They argued that the right to national self-determination of the Irish people was being denied them, and that the unionist population did not have a right to veto this.

The SDLP, in their document, had condemned the IRA campaign, and stated that the real issue was the fact that the Irish people were divided on how to exercise national self-determination, and that agreement between the two traditions could not be gained by the use of force. They argued that the British now played a neutral role in Northern Ireland, and that the Anglo-Irish Agreement, in which the British stated they would facilitate a united Ireland if the majority in Northern Ireland expressed a wish for that, was proof of this British attitude. During this meeting, the Sinn Féin delegates accused Hume of trying to change the object of the talks to being 'an end to all military activity in the North of Ireland'. It was agreed that both sides would produce more documents clarifying points raised in the earlier documents.

At a meeting held on 19 May, the republicans handed over a document in which they argued that the democratic rights of the unionist people must not extend to a veto over the national rights of the Irish people as a whole. The SDLP produced no document at that meeting, but handed over two papers when the delegations met again on 13 June. They argued that the 'real question' was how to end the British presence while at the same time leaving a peaceful and united Ireland behind, and that the answer was to unite the people of Ireland first. The challenge was to persuade the unionist people to join in a united Ireland. The republicans in turn suggested that the two nationalist parties unite in calling for a British withdrawal.

The issues of the position of the British government and the rights of the unionist population were points on which the two parties had obvious differences, and ones which were showing little sign of being reconciled. The two party leaders met again on 11 July to discuss progress. Another SDLP paper was handed to Adams, in which they argued that the neutral role of the the British government in Northern Ireland meant that the IRA's campaign was no longer legitimate, given the republicans' own criteria for legitimacy.

The delegations met again on 14 August and Adams handed a letter to Hume. He wrote that not much progress had been made but that the talks had been good for the morale of the nationalist community. He asked that the SDLP withdraw a reference to the 'natural right of veto' held by the unionists which appeared in one of the the SDLP documents. He said the statement 'seriously undermines nationalist presentation and perception of the six-county state as artificial'. In his view it still remained for the SDLP to be persuaded that the British occupation of Northern Ireland was the central problem and the first hurdle to be overcome. Finally, he did not consider the dialogue ended and hoped both sides would remain in regular contact.

A Broad Alliance

On 5 September both parties released statements 'on the end of the present round of Sinn Féin/SDLP talks', as Sinn Féin put it. In its statement, the SDLP made clear that its motive in getting involved in the discussions was an attempt to persuade the republicans to lay down their arms. 'Is the IRA doing anything to advance the interests of the population in whose name it claims to act?' they asked. The republican violence, or 'armed struggle' was wrong and even on its own terms was no longer justifiable (because of Britain's neutrality). 'We have asked the question therefore, is the method now more sacred than the cause?...'

'To those who claim the heritage of Pearse and Connolly we say: what would they do in your place? They laid down their arms to prevent the further needless suffering of their people. Will you not do the same?'

They posed the question to every member of the Provisional Republican Movement – if the SDLP was correct about the British position, then did they agree that this removed the stated justification for the 'armed struggle' of the IRA? 'The SDLP hopes and expects that the debate on these crucial issues which has begun will continue in the public and private arena, particularly among all those who regard themselves as republicans, and that it will lead sooner rather than later to an end of the agony of all the people of the North.'

The Sinn Féin document released on the same day contained a lengthy statement by Adams, but there was no direct mention of the IRA. Adams stated that from the outset Sinn Féin forwarded the view that the root cause of the conflict in Ireland was to be found in the British government's denial to the Irish nation of its right to national self-determination. This view was the 'consistent republican and democratic view'. While both parties agreed that the Irish people as a whole had the right to national self-determination, 'the Sinn Féin delegation was somewhat perplexed that the SDLP continues to maintain that the British government is now a neutral party to the conflict in Ireland'. That claim, Adams wrote, ignores all the historic evidence and was contradicted by the events of the previous twenty years. As evidence of this neutrality, the SDLP could only point to Article 1 of the Anglo-Irish Agreement 'despite the fact that the loyalist veto is explicitly contained within this article, despite the fact that the British government asserts that the Treaty is a "bulwark" against a United Ireland and despite the fact that even Charles Haughey recognised the Treaty to be a "copperfastening of partition"'.

Adams then turned an analogy based on the situation in Cyprus, and raised by Hume, to the republican advantage. 'To confer neutrality on the British government would be to confer neutrality on the Turkish government whose military invasion has partitioned the island of Cyprus.' Sinn Féin, he stated, was dismayed to discover that within the SDLP policy of 'unity by consent' was a 'recognition and acceptance of the loyalist veto'. This was an untenable position for a party that claimed to act in the interests of Irish nationalists. However, Sinn Féin did concur with the SDLP in stating that 'the real question is how do we end the British presence in Ireland in a manner which leaves behind a stable and peaceful Ireland... We firmly believe that the broadest possible alliance, informal or otherwise, of nationalists, republicans, socialists, and democrats in active and constant pursuit of a political solution which finds its basis in the democratic principle of national self-determination, is the best means of expediting the achievement of peace and justice in Ireland'. It was an idea to which the republicans were to give increasing emphasis.

'Undiluted Fascism'

At the end of the following November Hume addressed his party's annual conference and launched an attack on the IRA. In many ways it was an epilogue to the discussions with Sinn Féin and received extensive media coverage. He opened his speech with a reference to the proud traditions of the Ulster Protestants and called on them to have the self-confidence to sit down and negotiate a way of living together peacefully with the other tradition. Unionists could no longer live apart, in an archaic supremacism, he said, and then, having attacked the traditional unionist isolationist attitude, Hume turned his sights on the republicans.

> Self-determination of the Irish people is their objective, they say. The Irish people are defined by them, if we judge by their actions and their contempt for the views and opinions of other Irish people, as themselves alone.

That deep-seated attitude, married to their methods, had all the hallmarks of undiluted fascism, he continued. They had also the other hallmark of the fascist – the scapegoat – the Brits were to blame for everything, even their own atrocities! They know better than the rest of us. They know so much better that they take unto themselves the right, without consultation with anyone, to dispense death and destruction. By destroying Ireland's people, they destroy Ireland.

> I had discussions with them recently. The talks were designed to explore whether they were willing to lay down their arms and join the rest of the people of this island in the lengthy and difficult search for peace based on real self-determination. I put some questions to them about the price of their means and method, about the consequence of victory for their viewpoint, about peaceful alternatives which already exist. They replied with sheaves of paper reiterating well-worn declarations about nationhood and the rights of the Irish people to self-determination, while ignoring the single most self-evident fact that strikes every human being in the world as they look in at Ireland – the Irish people are divided on that very question, the question of how to exercise self-determination.

Hume then made the same charge against the republicans as he had earlier to the unionists – that they lacked the confidence to sit around a conference table and persuade their fellow Irishmen of their vision for a better Ireland. He then went on to criticise the military campaign and detailed the casualties of the last twenty years. In the twenty years up to the previous Saturday, 2,705 people had died. 44 per cent of these had been killed by the PIRA and 18 per cent by their 'fellow travelling "republican" paramilitaries'. 55 per cent of those killed were ordinary civilians and 69 per cent of them came from the Catholic community. In the past twenty years, republicans had killed more than twice as many Catholics as the security forces, and in the last ten years they had killed more than the loyalists, Hume said.

He then went on to describe the harassment which the nationalist population endure from the security forces and said that this would not exist if it were not for the IRA campaign. An ending of that campaign would lead to the end of the extraordinary security situation in Northern Ireland and a slow emptying of the prisons. Investment in the six counties could be attracted, and jobs created. But Sinn Féin refused to see the logic of this, he said, and failed to take responsibility for their own actions. Instead they blamed the British for everything and refused to recognise that the British position on Northern Ireland had changed.

Adams replied to Hume in the next edition of *An Phoblacht*.

Hume's analysis was flawed on a number of central issues, he wrote. His assertion that the British were now neutral was 'patently incorrect', as was his analysis of loyalism. 'Mr Hume claims that the Hillsborough Treaty has ended the unionist veto. Where is the proof of that? Every prominent Tory minister has reiterated that Hillsborough guarantees partition in perpetuity.'

Hume's claim that the republicans absolved themselves of their responsibilities and blamed everything on the British, Adams accused of being a gross misrepresentation of all they had said to the SDLP during their talks and also of the IRA's position. 'When [IRA] actions lead to civilian casualties or fatalities, the IRA is honest in accepting responsibility for such disasters as it is when the actions have the result which the IRA planned for,' Adams wrote. 'The IRA has clearly accepted the consequences of its actions.'

Adams then criticised Hume for using the occasion of his party's conference for solely attacking his political opponents, and for missing the opportunity for building a consensus on some of the issues which emerged during their talks. 'John Hume could, for example, have explained what the SDLP leadership means by unity by consent. Is it 50 per cent of the Six-County vote plus one? Is it an overall nationalist majority in the Six Counties? Is it 50 per cent of the unionist electorate plus one?... This was one of the questions put by Sinn Féin to the SDLP during our talks. We are still awaiting a reply.'

He ended his article as follows:

Three years ago Sinn Féin warned the SDLP that the Hillsborough Treaty would resolve nothing, would prolong the nationalist night-mare and would rapidly become a political millstone. At that time there was a golden opportunity to push, in conjunction with all shades of national and international opinion, for Irish independence. John Hume and his Dublin partners settled for the Hillsborough Treaty. Three years on, no amount of bluster can disguise their mistake.

12: Twenty Years of Fighting

In 1981 the year of the hunger-strikes, 101 people died in the violence in Northern Ireland. Over half of these were civilians. In subsequent years the numbers killed in the fighting dropped steadily, reaching the lowest figure since 1970 in 1985, when fifty-four people lost their lives. Twenty-four were 'civilians', with that figure including five IRA members, and twenty-three members of the RUC. Only two were British army (non-UDR). The war was successfully being 'Ulsterised'. However, in 1986 the numbers killed in the violence increased, and did so again in 1987, when a total of ninety-three people died. This increase can be accounted for by the rise in the number of civilian victims, caused by a wave of sectarian killings by loyalist paramilitaries – due, at least in part, to opposition to the Anglo-Irish Agreement – and the deaths from the Enniskillen bombing.

1988 began with warnings of an all-out offensive by the IRA who were believed to be heavily armed, having received large shipments of guns, ammunition and Semtex, the powerful explosive which does not register on normal security detectors from Libya. There were also reports of the IRA having surface-to-air-missiles, which if true would greatly endanger the British army personnel who travelled almost exclusively in helicopters in such border areas as South Armagh. Although these missiles were not used, 1988 was still to see the highest non-UDR British army death toll in many years.

The Gibraltar Killings

On 6 March 1988 three unarmed Provisional IRA members were walking towards the Spanish border after one of them had parked a car in central Gibraltar, when they were shot dead by plain clothes SAS troops. The soldiers had been flown to the colony specifically to deal with the Provisionals whose movements the British were aware of. It was suspected that the three were planning a bomb attack in Gibraltar and later a massive bomb was found in a car belonging to them, in an underground car park in Spain. It was believed that the car left in Gibraltar was being used to 'book a space' for the car bomb, which would be put in place in time for an expected army parade.

The three republicans who were killed instantly in the SAS attack were all senior members of the IRA. Daniel McCann, of Cavendish Street in the Lower Falls, was, according to the RUC, a prominent member of the Belfast Brigade, who had come to the fore following the rejuvenation of the Brigade after the 1986 crisis, when senior members had been expelled for criticising the low level of activity. The police believed he had taken part in many bombings and killings in the year prior to his death. His name had become known to loyalist paramilitaries, who had placed him near the top of their assassination list. A year before his death, men disguised as police officers called to his home in what is thought to have been a murder bid.

Seán Savage, of Downfine Gardens, Belfast, was considered to have been one of the top bomb-makers in the Belfast Provisionals, and Mairéad Farrell, of Stewartstown Road, Andersonstown, had been a prominent prisoner in Armagh Jail, where she served ten years for her involvement in a bombing, and had stood for election in Cork during the 1981 hunger-strikes. She had been released in August 1986, and had returned to the IRA.

The deaths caused a political storm, with allegations that the three had been gunned down without a chance to surrender, and that it had never been intended to take them alive. The British Department of Defence and the Foreign Office were accused of disinformation. A British TV documentary, which gave eye-witnesses' accounts which seemed to support the allegation that the three had been murdered, was the subject of an independent inquiry following expressions of outrage by the British government. At the subsequent inquests the men who shot the IRA members claimed they had shouted warnings to all three, but had started to shoot at them almost instantly because they moved their arms and were suspected to be reaching for triggers that would activate a suspected bomb in the parked car. The inquest failed to satisfy many who believed the killings were premeditated. But the deaths had more than just a political fall-out and were to lead to a further five particularly grisly killings.

A massive display of republican sympathy was organised for the return of the bodies of the three dead volunteers, which were flown into Dublin airport. Adams was among those present to receive them. A cortège brought the bodies to Belfast in a slow parade that the security forces on both sides of the border feared might lead to violence. However, the funeral parade passed off peacefully. That night Adams took the coverings off the three dead bodies.

The next day the coffins were brought to the republican plot in Milltown Cemetery, to be put lying beside the bodies of the many comrades who had fallen before them. Just after 1.30pm, as the third coffin was being lowered into its grave, a bearded man, armed with a handgun, lobbed a grenade into the crowd of some 10,000 mourners. Immediately there was shouting and screaming, and those who realised what was happening dived for cover. Gerry Adams grabbed a microphone and shouted to people to take cover, and tried to restore calm. Then there were another two explosions, and a burst of gunfire. The attacker was seen running down the slope of the cemetery towards the M1 motorway, and shouts went out to 'get him'. Adams called out over the microphone for ambulances and first-aid volunteers, as youths chased the gunman who ran towards the motorway, occasionally turning to shoot or lob a grenade at his attackers.

The gunman reached the motorway and fled southwards for about half a mile, all the time being chased by nationalist youths. When they drew close to him, he turned and lobbed a grenade, seriously injuring one of his pursuers. Two youths caught up with the man and knocked him over, and a blue Skoda car, which had been hijacked by three men, was driven into the attacker at speed. The crowd were shouting to 'gut him', but the three men in the car loaded him into the Skoda and sped off towards Belfast. His weapon was seized. The crowd shouted after the car that they wanted the man returned, so they could 'kick him to death'. The car disappeared but soon reappeared, speeding back towards the crowd. It stopped, and the three men jumped out of the car and dragged their captive after them, pulling him into a ditch where a group of men began to kick and beat him. However a fleet of RUC vehicles soon arrived and forced the crowd, at gunpoint, to hand over their captive and retreat back into the cemetery. The police made off with their prisoner.

Three young men died in the attack, and sixty-eight were injured. One of the injured was a boy of ten, another a mother of four who was seven and a half months pregnant. The three who died were Kevin Brady (30), Divis Flats, Thomas McErlean (20), Palestine Street, Ormeau Road, and John Murray (26), Moreland Park, Andersonstown. Unemployed builder Michael Stone (33), of Ravenswood Park, Belfast, was later convicted of the attack, as well as three other murders, six attempted murders, and three counts of conspiracy to murder prominent members of Sinn Féin. Stone claimed he worked in a 'freelance' capacity for various loyalist paramilitary groups. He had gone to the funeral in the hope of killing a number of prominent republicans, and had not wanted to injure or kill any women or children, he said.

It later emerged that Stone had wanted most of all to kill Adams and had, or so the gunman was to claim, at one point been so close to Adams that he had brushed up against him and decided he was wearing a light bullet-proof jacket.[1] The decision to kill Adams – and to kill Martin McGuinness – had been taken in the wake of the Enniskillen massacre, and the loyalists hoped that by killing the two they could spark a feud. An earlier attempt by Stone to kill McGuinness had been abandoned.

Only one of the three people killed in the cemetery attack, Kevin Brady, was a member of the IRA. On a Saturday afternoon, only three days after he had seen his comrades who had died in Gibraltar buried, Gerry Adams was again walking behind a coffin as it made its way towards the republican plot in Milltown Cemetery. And once again the solemn burial ceremony was to be transformed into a scene of rage and death.

The cortège had just left St Agnes' Church following Requiem Mass and was moving slowly behind a lone piper down Andersonstown Road when a car, a Volkswagen Passat, which had earlier ignored the directions of Sinn Féin stewards, suddenly emerged from a side-street at speed and drove towards the mourners. Inside the car were two plain clothes British soldiers, and what it was they were attempting to do was never to become quite clear. The wild antics of the car frightened and enraged the crowd, many of whom instantly assumed they were witnessing another loyalist attack. The soldiers, as they tried to extricate themselves from the midst of the republican funeral, were hemmed in by black taxis which were taking part in the procession, and instantly the VW Passat was surrounded by the outraged crowd. The car was overrun by youths who were kicking and beating at it, and trying to get at the two men inside. For a moment it seemed as if the stewards were about to gain control of the situation, but then one of the soldiers fired a shot in the air, and the crowd ran back from the car. One soldier began to climb out the window of his car, his revolver in his hand, but a man came up behind him as he did so and dragged him to the ground. Then the outraged crowd fell in on the car again and began to beat the two lost men furiously. Photographs were later to show that some of those who surrounded the car in anger had earlier been walking beside Kevin Brady's coffin.

One of the attackers was using an iron bar. 'We've got two Brits,' shouted some of the mourners. The two were dragged to nearby Casement Park, being punched and kicked all the way. There they were stripped to their underpants. The two unconscious and bloodied men were hauled to the top of a fifteen foot wall and thrown back down on the pavement, then put in a black taxi and taken to some waste ground at the rear of a row of shops on the Andersonstown Road. There they were both shot dead. The horrific assault on the car had been captured on video and by press photographers, and sent shock waves through the islands of Ireland and Britain, and across the world. A poignant picture of one of the soldiers, lying as if crucified on the patch of waste land, bloodied and stripped to his underpants, was later published in the newspapers.

The two dead NCOs were named as Corporal Derek Woods (24) and Corporal David Howes (23), and they were praised by their commanding officer Lt Colonel Martin Roberts for their 'remarkable restraint' in not using their weapons when under attack from an angry mob. If they had used their weapons it would have resulted in even further carnage, he said. The army insisted the two men were not on duty at the time, but had 'got lost'.

In a statement afterwards Sinn Féin described the deaths as 'terrible', and said that everyone believed there was going to be a repeat of the Milltown massacre when the soldiers' car drove into the cortège. 'Despite Sinn Féin's best efforts to restore calm, pandemonium broke out when the undercover soldiers produced their weapons. If those who are condemning what happened were there, what would they have done?' the statement asked.

The next day Fr Tom Toner delivered an emotional homily during Sunday mass in St Agnes' church, in which he said that the previous day's killings had been a parody on the Stations of the Cross, even down to the stripping. He had seen the image of Christ 'in the dead bodies that were sacrificed on the altar of hatred, revenge and fear... My dear people, what has happened to us? What have we got in our midst? What can we do?' he asked, and he called on his parishioners to pray.

The area of Andersonstown came in for strong vilification following the deaths, and newspapers wrote of how 'brutalised' the community had become, and there were assaults on the community as a whole, describing the people as 'less than human'. Adams spoke out in defence of the area, saying that the people there had suffered greatly, and that their reaction to the arrival of the two soldiers in their car had to be seen in the context of the Milltown attack.

The weapons taken from the two soldiers were later to be used in a number of killings of security force members by the IRA.

Targeting the British

In the early eighties the deaths of a number of republicans – and a civilian unconnected with any paramilitary group – had led to an outcry about a 'shoot-to-kill' policy which, it was alleged, a specially trained unit of the RUC had adopted. It was suspected by many that traps were set up by the police working on intelligence, and no attempt made to arrest republicans who entered these traps. Instead, they were shot down in a hail of bullets. A number of such instances led to the arrival of an investigating team from Britain to look into the alleged murders and when the man in charge of that inquiry, John Stalker, was removed from the task there was a political scandal which lasted for years.

The deaths at Loughgall and in Gibraltar were pointed to by republicans and others to support the allegation that such a 'shoot-to-kill' policy had also been adopted by the SAS. Substance to this allegation was given by the circumstances surrounding the death of an innocent civilian, a Belfast taxi driver Kenneth Stronge (47), who was killed by the security forces during a shoot-out between the SAS and an IRA unit attacking the North Queen Street RUC Station in early July 1988. Immediately after the gun and grenade attack from a hijacked Volvo car, shots rang out from behind the fortified walls of the police station. The security forces were aware of the impending attack, and an SAS unit was lying in wait for the republicans. The attackers, however, managed to escape. The SAS, because they were in 'hostile territory' were unable to hide a back-up unit outside the station. In the shooting Stronge, from Olympia Drive, South Belfast, was hit by army bullets, and died three days later from his injuries. It was speculated afterwards that the IRA unit may have managed to get away because the soldiers had waited until they opened fire before they, in turn, went into action. It was thought that this might be a policy change introduced following the controversy over the Gibraltar killings.

The IRA did not complain about the existence of a shoot-to-kill policy – it would be hard for them to do so considering their own policy towards members of the security forces, on or off duty. Rather, they used its existence as a counter argument against the British attempts to present the situation in Northern Ireland as something other than one of insurgency. Margaret Thatcher had met the coffins of the two soldiers who had died during the Brady funeral, when they were flown to a British army base in Britain. It was unusual for her to do so, but the deaths of these two soldiers had been more public and caused greater disgust and sorrow than most British army deaths. For the IRA, the picture of the British premier standing on the tarmac to show her respect at the return of the bodies of soldiers who had died in the conflict in Northern Ireland, was something of a propaganda coup. That, and a number of other issues which came to the fore during 1988, led to a marked increase in the number of British troops whose bodies were sent home following IRA attacks that year.

On 1 May the IRA carried out two attacks on British soldiers in Holland which left three dead and three seriously injured. The attacks, the IRA said, were intended to show that they still had the capability to carry out attacks on the British outside Northern Ireland. The three servicemen who died and the three who were injured were all stationed in West Germany and were on weekend leave in Holland at the time of the attacks. The IRA statement had the following message:

> We have a simple statement for Mrs Thatcher – disengage from Ireland and there will be peace. If not, there will be no haven for your military personnel and you will regularly be at airports awaiting your dead.

In June more than 200 British soldiers took part in a 'fun-run' in Lisburn, the site of the British army headquarters in Northern Ireland. About 4,000 people took part in the run, and thousands more packed into the town to spectate. However, as the run was taking place, an IRA unit placed a bomb under an unmarked blue military van, which was being used by a number of soldiers taking part in the event. After the race, as the soldiers made their way back to their barracks, the bomb exploded. The van burst into flames in the middle of the town, throwing the burning bodies of the soldiers out on to the street. Four died instantly, with another being dead on arrival at hospital, and a sixth dying a few hours later. At least ten people were injured in the blast. After the killings, Adams told *The Observer* newspaper that there were two reasons why the attacks on British soldiers were 'vastly preferable' from Sinn Féin's point of view, to the killing of members of the RUC or UDR. The first was the propaganda impact on political and public opinion in Britain. The second, he explained, was that 'callous as it may sound, when British soldiers die it removes the worst of the agony from Ireland'.

On 13 July the IRA bombed the British barracks near Duisburg, in West Germany, injuring nine soldiers. On 1 August a soldier was killed in an IRA blast at the Inglis Barracks in North London, right on the edge of the Prime Minister's constituency. On 5 August there was a blast at the British Roy Barracks near Düsseldorf, in which three soldiers and one woman civilian were injured. It was the fifth successful attack on British soldiers outside Northern Ireland since May, and led to more than 70,000 army personnel being virtually confined to barracks on 'Red Alert'.

That same week there were more killings in Northern Ireland, though they received less attention in Britain and elsewhere than the attacks on British bases in Britain and Germany. Off-duty UDR member Roy Butler was shot dead in front of his wife and two-year-old daughter outside a shoe shop in the Park Centre shopping mall, just off the Falls Road. Two elderly men, Fred Love and William Hassard, were murdered in a hail of bullets as they left Beleek RUC Station, having carried out routine maintenance work there. The IRA in West Fermanagh claimed responsibility for the attack, and said the workers had refused to heed numerous warnings not to do work for the British army or the RUC. Adams, in a newspaper interview, said he does not oppose this policy of killing workers who take up employment involving servicing the security force infrastructure in Northern Ireland. 'They did not have to take the contracts. There is a war going on and they took sides,' he stated.[2] On the same day Roy Butler was killed, an RUC officer died when a bomb which had been placed under his car exploded soon after he drove away from the police station in Lisburn.

A Coincidence of Tragic Accidents

The rush of attacks on the security forces was greeted in *An Phoblacht* with a front cover photograph of the blasted Inglis Barracks, and the large headline 'Resurgence'. It was a morale boost for the republicans after a line of 'mistakes' in which operations had resulted in the deaths of civilians, and the movement had come in for particularly strong vilification.

On 18 March an IRA unit lay in wait outside a house in Belleek, Co. Fermanagh, for a man whom, they claimed, was a member of the UDR. When a car appeared, they riddled it with bullets, killing young Gillian Johnson (21) outside her farmhouse home, and seriously injuring her fiancé. The IRA said later that the intended target was the dead woman's brother, who was in the UDR. But they were wrong in this also, as the man was not a member of the security forces.

Three months later, on the morning of 28 June, a bomb exploded on a schoolbus in Co. Fermanagh which had thirteen children on board. The driver of the bus was a part-time member of the UDR, and the intended target of the bomb. The bomb had been placed in the engine compartment, and the bus had been driven some six miles towards Enniskillen, before it exploded. The bomb inflicted severe chest and arm injuries on a fourteen-year-old girl, Gillian Latimer, who most likely would have lost her life if she had not been given first aid by the driver of the bus, who was himself badly injured in the blast.

The IRA expressed regret at the injury of the girl, the third time since November that they had apologised for an action in Co. Fermanagh. These incidents had all, however, been approved by Brigade staff and were an indication of the difficulties members of the IRA seemed to have with implementing the policies of carrying out only operations that would not under-mine efforts to expand the support base north and south of the border.

On 7 July, Eamonn Gilroy (24) from Lady Street, West Belfast, and Elizeabeth Hamill (60), from Clonard Rise, off the Falls Road, were walking past the swimming pool on the Falls Road when an IRA bomb designed to hit a joint army-RUC patrol, was detonated and killed them both. Four other people were injured in the blast, including a four-year-old girl and her grandmother. The IRA later accepted responsibility for the blast which had 'gone tragically wrong'.

Early the next day during the follow-up operation, British army bomb disposal officer John Howard stepped on a pressure plate and was blasted to death. He was the four hundredth British soldier to lose his life in the conflict in Northern Ireland.

In an interview a week later Adams said the run of civilian deaths and casualties was 'an unfortunate coincidence of tragic accidents' and rejected rumours that they were evidence of oppo-sition within the IRA to the ballot box and armalite strategy.[3] He said that the policy of avoiding civilian casualties must be rigor-ously implemented by IRA units, but declined to say why this was not occurring:

> The IRA has to accept the responsibility. The onus is on the IRA to minimise the risk to non-combatants. My position is quite clear. I would like to see operations in which there's a minimum risk to civilians and that hasn't obviously been the case in some recent operations. That's what I mean by the IRA putting its house in order. The IRA have to

pursue the armed struggle in such a way that it helps either to broaden the base or doesn't obstruct the broader aims of the movement.

This was all the more important given Sinn Féin's objective of wooing grass roots SDLP and Fianna Fáil supporters. On the Falls Road deaths he said the tragedy had 'brought home to the whole community and presumably to the IRA the thin line on which they thread, that the heart can be knocked out of the people and that confidence can be undermined in the very community of which the IRA is an integral part'.

Trying to broaden the base did not lay any restrictions on the IRA as they pursued the armed struggle, he said, all it did was reinforce restrictions which already existed. He also hinted that in the future the organisation would put more effort into killing British troops rather than members of the UDR or RUC:

> It is a fact which the Dublin establishment might not like to admit, but there is also a broad acceptance in the 26 counties which straddles all political parties that people don't have any problem about operations against British crown forces and particularly against what you would call British army units which are not domestically recruited – no problem whatsoever. Whilst people's tolerance might range from a tolerance to an actual applauding, the fact is that the sentiment is there…. If you start off from the basic position that this is morally the right way to do it and add all these other considerations then not only is it the right thing to do but it's also the clever thing to do – to pursue the armed struggle in such a way that it helps either to broaden the base or doesn't obstruct the broader aims of the movement.

Just seven days after the interview was published a Co. Down couple and their six-year-old son were driving home from the airport after a holiday in the United States, when an IRA roadside bomb was detonated and the family blown to pieces. The Shogun jeep in which they were travelling was totally destroyed by the bomb which was hidden in a derelict building beside the road at the border crossing at Killeen, the scene of the death of Judge Gibson and his wife in an IRA trap the previous year. Only the wheels of the vehicle in which Robert Hanna (44), his wife Maureen (44) and their son David, were travelling survived in any recognisable form after the massive blast, and they were found in a field some distance away from the tragedy.

The IRA accepted responsibility for the 'very carefully planned military operation which ended in most unfortunate circumstances'. It later emerged that the Northern Ireland High Court judge, Ian Higgins, had been on the same plane as the Hanna family, and like them was to drive from Dublin Airport up to Belfast. The judge had been travelling in a vehicle similar to that of the Hannas, and it is thought that the IRA blew up the Hannas' car believing it to be that of the judge. The killings brought to eighteen the number of civilians killed by the IRA in nine months.

However, in the weeks following the Adams interview the IRA launched its series of successful attacks against British troops and bases in London and on the continent. Just a week after the Inglis Barracks death and the attacks on the British quarters in West Germany, Sergeant Major Richard Michael Heakin (38), was shot dead by two IRA gunmen as he sat in his car waiting for the traffic lights to change just outside the port of Ostend, in Belgium. He was in civilian clothes and on his way to catch the ferry to England, where he was to visit his family in Wiltshire. He was the victim of an 'opportunistic' killing. The two gunmen had sat on a bench by the traffic lights, waiting for a car owned by a member of the British military – recognisable by their distinctive number plates. When Richard Heakin drew up at the traffic lights the two men walked up to the car and shot him at point blank range through the passenger window, and then ran off into a nearby park.

A week later, on Saturday, 19 August, the IRA delivered their greatest single blow to the British army since the massacre of eighteen troops in the 1971 bomb blast at Narrow Water, near Warrenpoint, Co. Down. A fifty-two seater bus carrying thirty-eight young British soldiers back to their barracks in Co. Down after a holiday break, was travelling along the Ballygawley-Omagh road in Co. Tyrone when a massive roadside bomb was detonated. The explosion blew a crater twelve feet in diameter and six feet deep in the road, and shattered the bus in which the troops were travelling. Dead bodies and injured men were scattered along the dark country road. 'It was completely black and all you could hear was screaming. The screaming was coming from the roadside, from the bus, from everywhere,' a local farmer who had been quick to the scene said afterwards. 'There were bodies everywhere. All young men. Young innocent men. It was heartbreaking.'[4] Eight soldiers were killed in the blast, all privates and unmarried. The youngest was eighteen, the oldest twenty-one. Twenty-eight others were injured.

There was an immediate crisis meeting of northern security chiefs, and Northern Secretary, Tom King, cut short his holiday and returned to the six counties to attend the emergency meeting. British Prime Minister Margaret Thatcher returned from Cornwall where she was on a brief holiday, to host a 'war council' in Downing Street. The attack was claimed by the East Tyrone Brigade of the IRA, the group which had lost many of its senior members at Loughgall the year previously. The deaths brought to twenty-seven the number of troops killed since the beginning of the year.

The wave of killings during August and most especially the bombing of the soldiers' bus totally transformed the morale of the IRA, which had been brought low by the series of 'mistakes' and outrages involving civilian casualties which began with Enniskillen. Now they had the Northern Secretary and the British Prime Minister cutting short their holidays to host crisis security meetings, and the campaign in Northern Ireland was once again the number one issue in the British media. Some members of the IRA believed that the introduction of internment – which many loyalist and British politicians were calling for, and which Adams had been warning might be introduced ever since the signing of the Anglo-Irish Agreement – would now occur, and would be followed by an escalation in the violence in the six counties. But when the British struck, it was not with internment, but with a more final method of removing suspected paramilitaries.

Only eleven days after the British army coach was blown to pieces on the Omagh-Ballygawley road, three senior IRA members met their deaths only a few miles away from the earlier tragedy. Brian Mullin, and brothers Gerry and Martin Harte, drove into a trap on the main Omagh-Carrickmore road in the Drumnakilly townland in Co. Tyrone on the afternoon of 30 August. The three men had earlier hijacked a Cortina car outside Omagh, and travelled to the scene of their deaths with the apparent intention of carrying out an attack on a member of the security forces, whom they believed to be driving a lorry in the area. When they drove up beside the parked lorry and opened fire, they were instantly killed in a hail of bullets from the SAS troops who were hiding in surrounding hedgerows and in a nearby derelict house. The scene of the deaths was instantly sealed off by squads of heavily armed troops as the sound of the shots died away.

Local priest John Cargan administered the Last Rites to the three dead men. One of the men was barely recognisable, such was the extensiveness of the wounds they had received. 'There were a considerable number of bullet holes in the car...irrespective of who they are, no one deserves to die this way.' All three of the dead men were well known to the security forces and suspected active IRA members. Both the Harte brothers, from nearby Loughmacrory, were married and both had one child. Brian Mullin, from Six Mile Cross, was single. It was reported that he was one of those taken in for questioning following the coach bomb killings, and he was a man named to Mrs Thatcher as a top IRA suspect by unionist MP Ken Maginnis when he met with the British Prime Minister following the Ballygawley road bombing. Mullin's sister was married to Martin Harte. According to the RUC, Gerard Harte (29), who was an architect, was a 'ruthless and dedicated terrorist' and was known to have been involved in a string of IRA operations in the area. They also claimed he was the commanding officer of the IRA in the area. Martin Harte (22) was said by the police to have been the local brigade's intelligence officer, responsible for 'targeting' soldiers and policemen for assassination. He had also been held for questioning after the Ballygawley road bombing.

The day after the killing of the three senior IRA men in Drumnakilly, the IRA suffered another setback, this time another operation which led to the deaths of civilians in a republican heartland. An elderly man and woman who went to check on a neighbour were blown to pieces when they opened a door which the IRA had booby-trapped.

Sheila Lewis, a 60-year-old widow, and Seán Dalton, a 55-year-old widower, had gone to check on a young neighbour in their flat complex in the Creggan area of Derry. The man who lived in the flat had not been seen for a few days. Mr Dalton entered the flat through a front window and went to open the door to let Mrs Lewis in. The door exploded bringing a shower of rubble down on the dismembered body of Mr Dalton, and throwing Mrs Lewis over the balcony railings to the ground below. It later emerged that the IRA had taken the young man from his flat some days earlier and were holding him in the Bogside. In a statement, the IRA said the intended target of their 'carefully planned' operation was a British army search party, and they apologised for the deaths.

The rate of killing in the six counties dropped as autumn approached. The IRA's campaign, despite their reported large store of weaponry and ammunition, was eased off, but there were to be further tragedies before the end of the year. On 26 October a bomb was placed under the wrong car by an IRA unit at Tomb Street in Belfast. The device exploded and killed Wilson Smyth, a 36-year-old Post Office employee. A month later there was yet more carnage in Co. Tyrone. Young Emma Donnelly and her 69-year-old grandfather, school traffic warden Barney Lavery, were killed when a huge IRA van bomb exploded as they drove past the unmanned RUC station in Benburb, Co. Tyrone. The car they were driving in was blown into a nearby field. The two who were killed had just left a bingo session. Friends described them as inseparable and it was reported afterwards that young Emma had recently written a school essay in which she described her grandfather as 'one of the most important people in her world'. The East Tyrone Brigade of the IRA claimed responsibility for the bomb. They said they had issued a warning but it had not been acted upon swiftly enough. The RUC refused to comment.

The deaths of young Emma and her grandfather brought to eighteen the number of civilians killed by the IRA since the beginning of the year. Loyalist paramilitaries, in their ongoing wave of sectarian killings, had killed twenty-one people in the same period, among them a UDR captain they mistakenly took for a Catholic. In addition, thirty-eight members of the security forces in the North had been killed by the IRA. It was just seven days after the deaths in Benburb that John Hume delivered his strong attack on the IRA, in which he said that the supposed defenders of the Catholic community in Northern Ireland had in recent times killed more members of their own community than either the security forces or the loyalist paramilitary groups. On the last day of 1988 the IRA, in a statement, admitted that it had been a bad year for them, with many of their members being killed, and many innocent civilians, including Catholics, dying 'in tragic circumstances at our hands'. But it warned the security forces that there would be no hiding-place for its 'gunmen and gunwomen' and that in 1989 there would be no place in Northern Ireland where they would be safe. The New Year, they announced, would witness 'consolidation of the struggle against the British'.

The Death of Harry Keyes

Despite the expression of concern the new year began with another civilian death at the hands of the IRA. The effect of the killing on the attempts by the republican movement to increase their support base in the twenty-six counties was all the greater due to the fact that the death occurred a few miles over the border, in Co. Donegal. Harry Keyes (25), a farm labourer from Ballycassidy, near Enniskillen, had been dating Anne Friel, from Racoo, Ballintra, Co. Donegal, and had paid numerous visits to his girlfriend's family home. In the months before Christmas he had been warned by the police that it was dangerous for him to be travelling across the border, and that his life might be in danger. Keyes had been a member of the RUC reserve, but had left three years previously. He continued to make visits to Donegal after the warnings, though less frequently. On the day of his death he had visited his girlfriend's mother in Racoo, and the couple had then gone walking at Rossnowlagh beach, five miles away. They then went to the nearby village, and got sweets for Anne's ten-year-old brother, Joseph, before returning to the Friel family home. Just after 8pm the couple were reversing out of the Friel driveway when they were confronted by their attackers. The gunmen fired one shot through the windscreen before ordering Anne out of the car. Then, at point blank range, they fired a number of shots into Harry Keyes as he sat in the driver's seat of the blue Cavalier car. 'Help me, help me,' he shouted as the gunmen shot him dead, and his girlfriend looked on helplessly. The men who carried out the attack shouted with excitement as they ran away.

The killing was claimed by the West Fermanagh unit of the IRA, a group that the gardaí said operated from bolt holes in the Bundoran area of Co. Donegal. Police on both sides of the border said the unit was responsible for a number of atrocities stretching back to the bombing at Enniskillen in November 1987, which some said they had been involved in. 'I cannot go into specifics but these people have the blood of many innocent victims on their hands,' an RUC officer told the Dublin-based *Evening Press*, which carried a front page story headed 'Get Donegal Murder Gang' on the day after the killing. The Dublin newspapers gave increased exposure to the story because it had taken place in the jurisdiction of the Irish government. Claims by the unit involved that the man had been killed because he had been gathering intelligence were discounted by almost everyone. The killing was seen a nakedly sectarian attack and the fact that it had taken place in front of the man's girlfriend, and that the killers seemed to have been elated by the experience, added to the horror felt by people afterwards. It was yet another disaster for the republican movement. Its negative impact was to hang over the 1989 Sinn Féin Ard Fheis which was held in the Mansion House in Dublin at the end of January.

A Broad-Based Front

The Ard Fheis had in fact been delayed, held back to take place on the seventieth anniversary of the 'First Dáil' which was the result of the 1918 pre-partition election that returned a majority of Sinn Féin candidates for Ireland as a whole. That Dáil had adopted a number of radical policy objectives which had since become an important part of the republican tradition, and one to which Adams often referred. However, unlike 1919, the 1989 gathering was not to be an exciting or ebullient affair. Since April 1987 the IRA had lost twenty-five volunteers, fourteen of them in SAS ambushes, and quite a number of those killed had been experienced and valued operators. Large poster photographs of fourteen of these dead IRA people adorned the walls of the hall during the Ard Fheis. Moreover, in the last three months of 1988 the RUC had arrested up to seventeen suspected IRA men, and all of them were in custody facing charges, some of them serious, which would ensure their being out of action for quite some time. During the three days of the gathering a number of speakers expressed the wish to see the struggle end soon.

In the week before the Ard Fheis *An Phoblacht* carried a front page story based on an IRA interview. 'Armed struggle will not compromise political struggle' ran the headline over the story, in which the IRA spokesperson spoke of one of the issues which has marred the past year – the deaths of civilians at the hands of the IRA. There was 'a greater realisation than ever of the need for the IRA to avoid civilian casualties', the spokesperson continued, particularly following the past year in which 'through a combination of tragic circumstances many civilians died in operations which dented the confidence of some of our supporters'. They went on to say that the IRA must now 'define our activities so that they do not hinder but complement efforts to build a broad-based front against imperialism', and warned that 'whilst the leadership is responsible to the broad republican movement for the consequences and repercussions of IRA actions, all volunteers are subject to the leadership for their conduct of the war'.

The article opened with a statement that the unit responsible for the death of Harry Keyes had been disbanded and disarmed. The unit had been disbanded not for any ulterior political motive, but because the killing of civilians was 'wrong, full stop', Sinn Féin Vice President, Martin McGuinness, was to say in an address to the Ard Fheis. 'The killing of non-combatants hurts and demoralises the struggle of people who have had to live for so long with injustice in this country. We must not, in challenging British rule, be the initiators of further injustice', he said, and added that the IRA had accepted responsibility for civilian deaths, unlike the British army which had yet to accept responsibility for the massacre in Derry on Bloody Sunday, seventeen years previously. The gardaí said later that they believed the Donegal unit concerned to be still active and armed, though the two members who had been responsible for the Keyes death had been court-martialled and expelled.

The creation of a broad-based front against imperialism as mentioned by the IRA spokesperson was the major item of Sinn Féin strategy debated at the Ard Fheis. Numerous speakers who supported the motion said that Sinn Féin 'could not win the struggle on their own'. Adams, in speaking for the motion, said that republicans had to go to the people and tell them that they wanted to work with them. 'Sinn Féin alone cannot win the struggle,' he said. The General Secretary of the party, Tom Hartley, who had proposed the motion for the establishment in principle of a 'broad anti-imperialist mass movement', said that its adoption marked a watershed in republican politics. Sinn Féin was acknowledging that it did not hold the holy grail on the national question, even if it was in the forefront of the struggle.

A Massive Responsibility

In his Presidential Address Adams referred to the 1988 talks with the SDLP and accused the moderate nationalist party of having 'lost their nerve' during the course of the discussions. They had claimed that Britain was now neutral in relation to its presence in Ireland, but when the republicans had called for this to be put to the test – by attempting to convince the British of adopting a policy objective of Irish independence – the SDLP had refused. This loss of nerve had meant that the discussions did not succeed in achieving the policy objective set by the anonymous third party.

Later in his address Adams said that since the previous Ard Fheis he had had a series of discussions with a number of Northern Protestants:

> These discussions crystallised for me the need for republicans to understand the perceptions and fears of this section of our citizens. The majority of Northern Protestants locked into their support for unionism and imperialism see the demand for Irish national independence as a demand for a creation of a Catholic state and an end to their Protestant identity. Many of them wrongly conclude when republicans call for a British withdrawal that we include them in that withdrawal scenario...
> Those perceptions, though foreign to Irish republicans, are held by many Northern Protestants. They represent a barrier which we must consistently try to break down. When we consider the gulf of pain and hate and the years of physical separation that exists between ourselves and the Northern Protestant population this is a formidable task. Yet it is one to which we must remain committed.

He devoted a greater bulk of his time to the IRA in his address than he had ever done before. He mentioned the members of the republican movement who had died since the previous Ard Fheis, and then went on to say that 'our sadness in the last year' was not confined to old comrades, but had also been caused by the 'exceptional and regrettable level of civilian casualties and fatalities arising from IRA operations'. Referring to the number of times he had spoken out against specific IRA actions in the past year, he said he was 'speaking for every Irish republican when I refused to condone those operations in which civilians were accidentally killed or injured. Our dismay, our regret and our sympathy with the plight of families bereaved by the IRA is genuine. The British crown forces can kill or injure civilians deliberately and with impunity. That is part of their policy. The IRA cannot. That has never been part of its policy, as the IRA itself has often reminded us'.

He reminded the delegates that when he was elected President he had elaborated on his attitude towards armed struggle as:

> a necessary and morally correct form of resistance in the Six Counties against a government whose presence is rejected by the vast majority of Irish people. This remains my position. I then went on to say: 'In defending and supporting the right of Irish people to engage in armed struggle it is important for those so engaged to be aware of the constant need and obligation to continuously examine their tactics and strategies. Revolutionary force – and this excludes sectarian violence – must be controlled and disciplined so that it is clearly seen as a symbol of our people's resistance.' I said these words in comradeship and in solidarity and in tribute to the freedom fighters of the IRA. Today, in that same spirit of comradeship, solidarity and tribute, I repeat those words.

Adams repeated the oft-quoted view that the history of British colonial involvement showed that the British government only understood the argument of force. In Northern Ireland, armed struggle 'sets the political agenda' and can help the overall struggle of the people. But the politics which shapes the struggle 'must guide and control the actions of that struggle'. He spoke of the damage civilian deaths did to the republican movement, and then addressed himself 'directly to the active service volunteers of Óglaigh na hÉireann (IRA)':

> You have a massive responsibility. At times the fate of this struggle is in your hands. You have to be careful and careful again. These are the feelings of the broad mass of the republican people, feelings which are

shared by republican activists and which now call for more circumspec-
tion than ever before. The morale of your comrades in jail, your own
morale and of your comrades in the field can be raised or dashed by your
actions. You can advance or retard the struggle.

He went on to say that he was

mindful that the media will misrepresent my remarks. I am aware that
the hardy annuals of unfounded speculation about hawks and doves,
splits and disagreements will be given yet another airing. For this
reason some of you may feel that some of those things should be left
unsaid. I understand such sentiment but it is a responsibility of leadership to lead from the front on this crucial issue as much as any other.
Nothing I say should be interpreted as condemnation of the IRA.
Smaoinimid agus brón orainn faoi na hÓglaigh a d'éag i mbliana. The
men and women volunteers of Óglaigh na hÉireann have my continued
loyalty. As I remind them of their responsibilities, I salute them as
freedom fighters.

Epilogue

At the 1986 Ard Fheis, when Sinn Féin voted to end abstention, Gerry Adams warned party members not to expect a breakthrough in the twenty-six counties in the next election. The second election after the ending of the policy of abstention would be the first true indicator of the effect that policy change had had, and that would show the success or otherwise that the party was having in building up its base.

That second election occurred in June 1989 when the Haughey minority government went to the country and, after failing once again to achieve a majority, formed a coalition government with the Progressive Democrats. The election was a major disappointment for Sinn Féin. Some members had been hoping that they would win a seat. However, the Sinn Féin vote dropped from 1.9 per cent to 1.2 per cent overall. This happened at a time when the governing party, Fianna Fáil, had introduced a series of cutbacks in public services and capital programmes in an effort to improve the health of the country's finances. The brunt of the hardships imposed by this policy had fallen on the poorer sections of Irish society, yet in the twelve constituencies contested, the percentage Sinn Féin vote was between one and three per cent.

Both the Labour Party and the Workers' Party gained votes and seats, securing an overall 15.1 per cent of the poll for the left. A considerable amount of the increased left vote came in Dublin. The Green Party surprised all observers and won a seat in Dublin South. 'Dublin Sinn Féin was in a state of shock after the last general election', Dublin party worker Owen Bennett was to say at the Ard Fheis the following February. 'There was a swing to the left yet we were unable to pick up on that.' He added that a post-election analysis had concluded that two of the factors leading to the lack of success of the party was the undue emphasis on the 'national question' and 'aspects of the Northern campaign'.

In the week before the 1990 Ard Fheis, sixteen-year-old Charles Love had died when hit by a piece of flying masonry in Derry after an IRA bomb had exploded during a commemoration march for those killed on Bloody Sunday. The bomb had been intended for members of the security forces.

In April 1989 Adams said in an interview that he did not know why the IRA had failed to heed warnings from himself and Martin McGuinness to avoid civilian casualties, but believed the problem to be 'a matter of great urgency'.[1] 'What is before us now – success or failure – depends on the issues we're talking about: the ability of the IRA to put its house in order and it's a matter of great urgency that the IRA do that.' He said he did not believe that Sinn Féin's support in the six counties was invulnerable to the effects of 'mistakes'. In the same interview he denied that there were those inside Sinn Féin who were questioning the validity of the IRA's campaign. 'I don't know of any who are asking about the value of armed struggle', he said. 'People are questioning the value of operations which do not advance the broad republican struggle but there is no questioning of the validity of the armed struggle which is being conducted minus the mistakes.'

At the February 1990 Ard Fheis Pat McKeown of the Ard Comhairle said accidents in the course of operations were a factor in the limitation of electoral support in Northern Ireland.

In the May 1989 local elections in Northern Ireland, the republicans managed to hold an overall percentage vote of 11.3 per cent, although there was an actual drop in the numbers who voted for them of 6,500. The same elections saw an increase in the SDLP vote. In the European elections in Northern Ireland in June the Sinn Féin vote fell from 13.3 to 9.15 per cent. In the Republic, Sinn Féin received only 1.1 per cent of the Euro-vote. They did not contest the seat in Munster, where republican priest Fr Paddy Ryan received a considerable vote but did not win a seat. In Connacht/Ulster their percentage vote dropped from 6.82 to 4.99. In Leinster the drop was from 4.32 to 2.64. In Dublin it was from 5.17 to 2.58.

During that year attempts were made to forge the broadly-based movement discussed at the February Ard Fheis. To mark the twentieth anniversary of the arrival of the British troops in Northern Ireland there was a large march in Dublin, organised by FADA, an umbrella group which included Sinn Féin. It was one of the largest marches seen in Dublin since the hunger-strikes, and ended outside the British embassy. Adams was among the speakers who addressed the crowd.

Some of the organisers believed it was a strategic mistake for Sinn Féin to have had their flute and drum bands from the six counties – which were such a notable part of the parade – take part in such a march. The bands had a noticeable paramilitary air, which it was thought caused something of a culture-clash with prospective supporters in the South. Adams voiced support for the IRA during his address to the crowd, which also caused considerable disquiet among some of the organisers, who considered the march to be in support of a united Ireland, but not of the IRA campaign.

During the 1990 Ard Fheis there was little talk or debate about the IRA. Unlike most previous conferences, there were no rallying cries, although it was the occasional emotive messages of support for those involved in the armed struggle which led to the greatest responses from delegates. There was no message from the IRA in *An Phoblacht* in the issue prior to the Ard Fheis, and Adams, in his Presidential Address, only referred to them briefly. On a number of occasions he referred to their continued ability to 'strike telling blows against the colonial regime' and to 'shatter the British propagandistic myth of the invincibility of the British army and its most elite regiments'. However he also seemed to voice continued concern about the effects of IRA 'mistakes'. The justness of the republican cause speaks for itself and must be guarded jealously, he said. 'It must never be undermined by any republican actions...we enjoy sufficient support to defend and advance the interests of our struggle if we do so intelligently.'

But there was little sign of any intention of calling a ceasefire. Having referred to a British strategy which was aimed at convincing Sinn Féin and the IRA of the futility of their efforts, a strategy which was aimed at using 'the length of our struggle against us', Adams continued:

> What should our response be? Should we retreat before this counter-offensive? Should we submit to revisionism, neo-colonialism and the perpetuation of British rule with all its evils? Does Thatcher expect us to say 'well we've done our best, what's the use, it's been a hard 20 years, there's no point in going on?' If by chance she and her cronies think this will be the the message from this Ard Fheis then once again they have got it wrong.

The main emphasis of the Ard Fheis were ideas expounded on in Adams' third book, *A Pathway to Peace*.[2] In this publication Adams considered the concept of national self-determination, and gave his analyses of the Hillsborough Accord, unionism, the role played by the Dublin government and by the SDLP and 'constitutional nationalists' in general. He also referred to the talks held between the SDLP and Sinn Féin. He wrote that the talks were the first example in recent times 'of dialogue between a section of constitutional nationalism and leading elements in the anti-imperialist struggle'.

The book contained a scathing criticism of constitutional nationalists. What the SDLP and constitutional nationalists in the Republic want, he wrote, is a situation – with partition still in existence – where they can further the interests of the nationalist middle-class in the six counties. He claimed that constitutional nationalists had no strategy for achieving Irish reunification, and that many politicians referred to it only because they could win votes that way – or would lose votes if they said they opposed it. While partition still existed it was not possible for the social or political aspirations of the majority of the nationalist population to be realised, wrote Adams. Yet what constitutional nationalists did was to try to control and limit the expression of political ambition of the nationalist population.

Adams then stated his view that the six counties, as a political unit, was basically flawed. 'The inequities which the six-county state has spawned are an inevitable consequence of its very existence', he argued. What was needed was an all-Ireland mass movement committed to Irish national self-determination. Such a movement, he wrote, would either cause the constitutional nationalists to get more actively involved for fear of losing support, or cause them to refuse to support the movement, and so be discredited. He also argued that national self-determination was an option which permitted unionists, minus their veto, to be involved in the shaping of their future on equal terms with all other Irish citizens. He suggested that a Charter, such as the one adopted by the African National Congress, could be drafted.

The concluding paragraph of his book read:

> We must begin to develop a programme for a movement which would appeal to all those capable of taking a national stand and which would require a multi-sided campaign of national regeneration. The building of such a movement is the urgent task of all socialists, nationalists and republicans. Irish national self-determination is the democratic option. It must be put on the agenda now.

It was the building of a vibrant Sinn Féin organisation, and of a movement such as that outlined above, which were the main concerns of the 1990 Ard Fheis. At the end of over a quarter century of fighting and campaigning, Gerry Adams was searching for a beginning.

Chapter Notes and References

CHAPTER 1

1. *Irish Times*, (Dublin), 16 March 1972.
2. MacStiofáin, Seán, *Revolutionary in Ireland*, Saxon House, Farnborough 1974, p. 269.
3. *Ibid.*
4. *Ibid.*

CHAPTER 2

1. Adams, Gerry, *Falls Memories*, Brandon Books, Dingle 1982, p. 129.
2. *Ibid.*, p. 134.
3. Adams, Gerry, *The Politics of Irish Freedom*, Brandon Books, Dingle 1986, p. 15.

CHAPTER 3

1. Adams, Gerry, *The Politics of Irish Freedom*, p. 32.
2. *Ibid.*, p. 33.
3. *Republican News*, (Belfast), 27 November 1976.

CHAPTER 4

1. *Republican News*, (Belfast), 27 November 1976.
2. MacStiofáin, Seán, *Revolutionary in Ireland*, p. 146.

CHAPTER 5

1. MacStiofáin, Seán, *Revolutionary in Ireland*, p. 146.

CHAPTER 6

1. *Irish News*, (Belfast), 20 and 21 July 1973.
2. Rees, Merlyn, *Northern Ireland: A Personal Perspective*, Methuen, London 1985, p. 162.
3. *Irish Times*, (Dublin), 20 July 1983.
4. Brigadier J. M. Glover, 'Northern Ireland: Future Terrorist Trends,' (unpublished). See Cronin, Seán, *Irish Nationalism*, The Academy Press, Dublin 1980, pp. 339-357.
5. *Republican News*, (Belfast), 8 May 1976.

CHAPTER 7

1. *An Phoblacht*, (Dublin), 2 September 1977.
2. *New Hibernia*, (Dublin), November 1979.

CHAPTER 8

1. *An Phoblacht*, (Dublin), 29 September 1979.
2. *An Phoblacht*, (Dublin), 27 October 1979.
3. Beresford, David, *Ten Men Dead*, Grafton Books, London 1987, p. 54.
4. *Ibid.*, p. 84.
5. *Ibid.*, p. 108.
6. *Ibid.*, p. 113.
7. *Ibid.*, p. 126.